Jesuit Studies

Contributions to the arts and sciences

by members of the Society of Jesus

JESUIT STUDIES

The Churches
and the Schools

AMERICAN PROTESTANTISM AND POPULAR

ELEMENTARY EDUCATION

Francis X. Curran, S.J.

LOYOLA UNIVERSITY PRESS

Chicago, 1954

The relations of the church and the state to education is now, and promises to remain, a much agitated question among Americans. Even while the present study was in preparation, a number of books and magazine and newspaper articles discussed the topic. Overlooked in these publications—as, indeed, in the general histories of American education—was a revolutionary development in the history of education and in the history of Christianity: the surrender by American Protestantism during the past century of the control of popular elementary education to the state.

This fact is unique in the history of Christendom. Traditionally, the Christian Church has claimed the right to exercise at least a measure of formal control over the education of its children. The Catholic Church still seeks to implement this claim. So, apart from American Protestantism, do the Protestant churches. Only in the United States has Protestantism relinquished the traditional claim of the Christian Church to exercise control over the formal education of its children in the elementary schools.

The fact of that unique development is too enormous to be completely ignored. But when educational historians have been perceptive enough to discern the fact, they have shown a massive unconcern in the investigation of its causes. The object of the present volume is to explore those causes.

6224

In the preparation of this work many debts of gratitude were incurred. Without the assistance of librarians, most of whom are nameless to the research worker, who could hope successfully to pursue historical research? They cannot be thanked by name; all the writer can do is gratefully to list the deposits in which research was done. Material for the present study was found in the following: Columbia University, Union Theological Seminary, General Theological Seminary, the New York Methodist Historical Society, the American Baptist Historical Society at Crozer Theological Seminary, Yale University, Harvard University, Andover Theological Seminary, the New York Public Library, and the Boston Public Library.

F. X. C.

October 4, 1953

CONTENTS

CHAPTER I

The Churches
and the Schools

In the course of its history Protestantism has developed several unique characteristics within the boundaries of the United States. One striking difference between the parent bodies in Europe and their offspring in America is the fact that the minor sects of Europe are the major denominations of the United States. On these western shores the tradition of Protestant dissent has come into its own.

In the nineteenth century a powerful and ultimately successful drive for universal education on the elementary level developed in western Europe and its overseas extensions. In European countries with a predominantly Protestant population—in the British Isles, Holland, Germany, and Scandinavia—this popular elementary education was entrusted largely to the control of the Christian churches. In North America denominational schools became the usual means of elementary instruction north of the Canadian border.

As American Protestantism departed from its European prototype in the marked growth of the American Evangelical denominations, so the Protestantism of the United States diverged from the European Protestant tradition of the control of education by the church. The connection between the two peculiarly American developments would appear to be more than casual.

Some Protestant churches, it is true, attempted to create and maintain denominational systems of elementary schools within the United States. A few denominations still carry on the effort.[1] But, by and large, American Protestantism has relinquished the age-old claim of the Christian Church to control the formal elementary education of its children.

History shows that, when once the principle of universal education is accepted as the ideal and aim of a nation, only two institutions have claimed the ability to implement that ideal and accomplish that aim. Organizations of parents or private educational institutions cannot hope to supply the rudiments of education to all the children of a nation. Popular elementary education must perforce be imparted by the church or by the state, working singly or together.

Since the time of the Protestant Revolt the state has increasingly entered upon and occupied fields once reserved to the church. Some examples that spring instantly to mind are the regulation of marriage, the supervision of vital statistics, the probation of wills, the care of the sick and aged, and the relief of the indigent. During the nineteenth century the state moved into the area of education; increasingly, its control of that area has been enlarged.

The intrusion of the state into a field hitherto occupied by the church was greeted by varied reactions from the various Christian denominations. The state, however, was not to be stayed. The exigencies of the new nationalistic state, tending towards democracy and liberalism and demanding a fervent devotion to the concepts of nationalism, required a citizenship educated in its new rights and its new duties. The Christian churches eventually agreed that the state must have an important place in the direction of popular elementary education.

---

[1] For a survey of these efforts see Edwin H. Rian, *Christianity and American Education*, pp. 202 ff. (San Antonio: Naylor Company, 1949).

The Catholic Church universally and the Protestant churches in Europe continued, however, to maintain the traditional claim of the Christian Church to control the elementary education of the young. It was in the United States that there occurred a revolutionary development in the history of Christianity and in the history of education. Not only did the American Protestant churches agree that the state had an important stake in popular elementary education, but these denominations went further and abandoned the educational traditions of the Christian Church. Voluntarily they relinquished the control of popular elementary education to the only other claimant, the state.[2]

This development within American Protestantism still remains unique. Anticlerical governments in lands usually called Catholic have frequently expelled the Church from the schools; but the Catholic Church has never voluntarily abandoned education to the state. In the twentieth century Nazi and communist totalitarianisms have destroyed the educational influence, not only of the Catholic, but of the Protestant and Orthodox churches. Before the outbreak of the Second World War the schools had been secularized in Germany and in Russia. The recent Red attacks on the schools of all the churches behind the Iron Curtain are common knowledge. Nor does it appear that the Protestant and Orthodox churches voluntarily relinquished the education of their children to the communist state.

While within the British Commonwealth some voices have been raised, urging the Protestants to follow the example of their American coreligionists, the English churches have continued to implement the traditional Christian position. In Eng-

---

[2] William C. Bower, *Church and State in Education*, p. 28 (Chicago: University of Chicago Press, 1944), contends that this surrender by the churches was reluctant. Conrad Moehlman, *School and Church: The American Way*, p. 13 (New York: Harper and Brothers, 1944), declares that Protestantism had relinquished education to the state before 1791. He then devotes his whole fifth chapter to a refutation of his own contention.

land itself Anglican, Catholic, and Nonconformist schools share with the board schools the function of imparting elementary education, and share likewise in the financial resources of the state. Apparently the English find that their multiple systems of primary schools imperil neither education nor democracy.

An interesting comparison might be made between the divergent developments on the control of education in the two great English-speaking democracies. Can the difference be attributed to greater English tolerance of religious pluralism and greater American concern for cultural unity? A simple affirmative to that question would be clearly wrong. Tentatively, however, some important elements in the problem may be suggested.

The drive for popular education in England was, in its earlier days, supported chiefly by the Established Church. The Anglican Church had a long tradition of control of education. The minority churches, Nonconformist and Catholic, were relatively less important than their branches in the United States. In particular, the Catholics were a small, quiescent group, who could scarcely be stigmatized as alien or anti-English. When, as late as 1870, legislation creating board schools was passed, the English were quite accustomed to church primary schools, and the children to be educated in the English schools were a homogeneous native group.

When the drive for universal education began in the United States, no single American church approximated the standing of the Church of England. Amid the welter of sects, the Evangelical denominations increasingly moved towards numerical predominance. Particularly in Evangelical Protestantism was the tradition of church-controlled education weak. Faced with the difficulty of sustaining many systems of parochial schools, the churches were persuaded to allow the state to control the schools, provided that they be, as they largely were, Protestant schools. Besides imparting the rudiments of learning, the elementary schools had the further function of creating a single nation out of disparate European strains. The Catholic Church, generally considered as alien and increasingly composed of aliens, was envisioned as a threat to this program of Americanization; consequently the movement toward state control of education was strengthened.

American Protestantism has handed over to the state its claim to control the primary education of children. What have been the consequences of that act? It is doubtful whether an adequate answer to the question can be given. And whether the consequences are considered praiseworthy or damnable will depend largely on one's viewpoint.

One consequence seems beyond doubt. Education, like history, is a whole. For the sake of convenience, both are divided into periods. The division of formal education into elementary, secondary, and higher sections is, in a true sense, as arbitrary and unreal as the division of history into ancient, medieval, and modern periods. If, then, a Christian church relinquishes its claims on any one of the divisions of formal education, it implicitly admits that it has no part in education. If a church withdraws from one division of education, the logical consequence of that withdrawal will be the ultimate abandonment of all formal education by that church.

During the nineteenth century American Protestantism gave up its claim to the formal control of elementary education. Today the logical consequences of that act have very largely worked out. The numerous Protestant academies and high schools of the past century have, for the most part, passed out of existence. Although large numbers of colleges established by the Protestant denominations are still in existence, many have passed completely out of the control of the churches, and many more maintain but an extremely tenuous connection with the founding denominations. Even in those colleges that are still dominated by the churches, the education imparted often does not differ notably from the education of secular colleges.

Another effect of the Protestant rejection of formal educational control was to enlarge the area of state control of American life. For many years the Protestant churches saw to it that the educational goals of the public schools were in accordance with their own aims. In recent years the aims of public education have been increasingly set by secularist teachers' colleges and educational associations. Has the increased secularization of public-school education fostered the obvious secularization of American life? Has the Protestant withdrawal from formal control unwittingly aided the drive of the secularists to expel all religious teaching from the public schools?

Other questions might be asked. Have the public schools, by refusing to teach the specific tenets of a particular church, contributed to the present Protestant questioning of dogmatic Christianity? Has public education thus prepared the ground for the growth of the Protestant ecumenical movement? To what extent have the American public schools lessened racial and religious tensions? Allowing for different circumstances, have they been more successful in this than, say, the church schools in England? One reason why Catholics support parochial schools is to keep their children faithful to their church. Have the public schools had an adverse effect on membership in the various Protestant churches?

Possibly a number of other pertinent questions might be posed; but whatever the questions and whatever the answers, it is a fact that the educational situation of the present day troubles many Protestant churchmen. Had their denominations taken a different stand in the day of decision, the United States might now possess parochial schools equal or superior in number and in pupils to the public schools of the civil government. Possibly American Protestantism may reverse the decision it has made on the question of the control of popular elementary education; but that improbable eventuality concerns, not the historian, but the prophet.

Since the story of the movement for universal elementary education in the United States has been recounted in all the general histories of American education, it need not be repeated here.[3] In reading these volumes one cannot but be aware that they were written by men who were more educators than historians, and educators, moreover, who were convinced of the supreme value of the state control of education. At times, indeed, the reader will appreciate the recent lament of an historian of education over the "decline and fall of educational history" because of the tendencies of historians of education "towards dogmatism, superficiality, repetitiousness and bombast."[4]

Historians agree that in colonial America the chief motive behind the establishment and conduct of schools was religious.[5]

---

[3] See, inter alia, Elwood P. Cubberley, Public Education in the United States, second edition, pp. 120 ff. (Boston: Houghton Mifflin Company, 1924), and his History of Education, pp. 653 ff. (Boston: Houghton Mifflin Company, 1920); Andrew S. Draper, American Education, pp. 17 ff. (Boston: Houghton Mifflin Company, 1909); Edgar W. Knight, Education in the United States, new edition, pp. 192 ff. (Boston: Ginn and Company, 1934); Paul Monroe, Founding of the American Public School System, pp. 183 ff. (New York: The Macmillan Company, 1940); Edward H. Reisner, Evolution of the Common School, pp. 319 ff. (New York: The Macmillan Company, 1930), and his Nationalism and Education since 1789, pp. 368 ff. (New York: The Macmillan Company, 1922); Newton Edwards and Herman G. Richey, The School in the American Social Order, pp. 322 ff. (Boston: Houghton Mifflin Company, 1947); Stuart G. Noble, History of American Education, pp. 149 ff. (New York: Farrar and Rinehart, 1938); John S. Brubacher, History of the Problems of Education, pp. 332 ff. (New York: McGraw-Hill Book Company, 1947).

[4] William W. Brickman, Guide to Research in Educational History, p. iii. New York: New York University Press, 1949.

[5] Besides the works cited in note 3 see Merle Curti, The Social Ideas of American Educators, pp. 4 ff. (New York: Charles Scribner's Sons, 1935); Herbert B. Adams, The Church and Popular Education, p. 14 (Baltimore: Johns Hopkins Press, 1900); Willard S. Elsbree, The American Teacher, pp. 32 ff. (New York: American Book Company, 1939). Samuel W. Brown, The Secularization of American Education, pp. 5 ff. (New York: Teachers College, Columbia University, 1912), brings together many colonial documents illustrating this point. For the secularization of public education through legal enactments see the documents cited by Burton Confrey, Secularism in American Education, pp. 47 ff. (Washington: Catholic University of America, 1931).

It was not until after the Revolutionary War that the idea was advanced that the control of formal education should be vested in the state rather than in the church.[6] Our purpose is not to trace the development of this idea, but rather to study the reactions of the churches to it; hence it will be sufficient to state that the pattern of elementary education had been set by the states of the North and West through legal enactments by 1850, or at the latest by 1860.

It was in the second quarter of the nineteenth century that the movement for universal elementary education first became of importance. The manuals commonly list, among the instruments which fostered interest in popular education, private school societies and infant, monitorial, and Sunday schools.[7] The general histories of education go on to mention various types of propaganda which proved effective, such as educational conventions and journals, reports, surveys, and memorials. Great stress is placed by the manuals on the work of leaders of the movement such as Horace Mann, Henry Barnard, Calvin Stowe, and many others.[8]

The histories of education also state that the drive for popular education profited from the humanitarian movement, the democratic movement, and the beginnings of American indus-

---

[6] Allen O. Hansen, *Liberalism and American Education in the Eighteenth Century* (New York: The Macmillan Company, 1926); Curti, *op. cit.*, pp. 34 ff.; Howard K. Beale, *History of Freedom of Teaching in American Schools*, pp. 47 ff. (New York: Charles Scribner's Sons, 1941); Elmer E. Brown, *The Making of Our Middle Schools*, third edition, pp. 204 ff. (New York: Longmans, Green and Company, 1907); Geoffrey O'Connell, *Naturalism in American Education*, pp. 43 ff. (New York: Benziger Brothers, 1938).

[7] See, for example, Cubberley, *Public Education in the United States*, pp. 149 ff., and Knight, *op. cit.*, pp. 160 ff.

[8] For the disputed stand of Mann on religious education see B. A. Hinsdale, *Horace Mann and the Common School Revival*, pp. 210 ff. (New York: Charles Scribner's Sons, 1898); Raymond B. Culver, *Horace Mann and Religion in the Massachusetts Public Schools*, pp. 217 ff. (New Haven: Yale University Press, 1929).

trialism, which were marked by the growth of cities and the creation of an industrial laboring class. The effect upon popular education of this last development, however, is subject to different evaluations.[9]

It may be noted that none of the general histories of American education attribute an influential part in the development of support for popular elementary education to the Protestant denominations. It is quite commonly believed that one of the effects of the Protestant Revolt was a demand for universal education. This demand, it is held, arose from the Protestant doctrine of the private interpretation of Scripture as the sole source of faith, from the Protestant attitude toward the Bible, and from the consequent necessity of teaching all men at least enough letters to read that Bible. Whatever validity that hypothesis may have, the historians of American education would appear to believe that it did not apply to the Protestant churches of nineteenth-century America.

The Bible, however, did prove a bone of contention in the history of American public schools. Catholic opposition to the use of the Protestant version of the Bible in purportedly nonsectarian common schools, as well as Catholic efforts to obtain public funds for their parochial schools, caused reac-

---

[9] Frank T. Carleton, *Economic Influences upon Educational Progress, 1820-1850*, p. 119 (Madison: Wisconsin University, 1908), finds that "the tax-supported, state-maintained public school is essentially an outgrowth of industrial evolution." Philip R. V. Curoe, *Educational Attitudes and Policies of Organized Labor in the United States*, p. 191 (New York: Teachers College, Columbia University, 1926), finds that organized labor contributed little to the growth of the demand for popular education.

There is also a difference of opinion on the stand of labor on organized religion and religious education in the public schools. Curoe, *op. cit.*, p. 42, and John Commons and others, *History of Labor in the United States*, I, p. 272 (4 vols., New York: The Macmillan Company, 1918-1935), find little opposition among labor. Sidney Jackson, *America's Struggle for Free Schools*, pp. 166 ff. (Washington: American Council on Public Affairs, 1941), would give antireligious feeling in laboring circles more weight.

tions, at times violent, among the Protestant denominations.[10] While many Protestants welcomed and sought subsidies from the civil governments for their secondary schools,[11] the Protestant churches almost unanimously opposed the grant of public funds to Catholic parochial schools.[12]

That the existence of Catholic parochial schools influenced Protestant opinion on the question of the control of popular elementary education is generally accepted. The Beards, for example, declare that the coming of large numbers of Catholic immigrants, who were "likely to fall under Catholic direction if educated at all in charity schools, frightened Protestants of every proclivity, making them willing to accept secularism rather than papal authority."[13]

The Protestant attitude toward Catholic parochial schools must necessarily come into consideration in this study, the aim of which is to discover the motives which induced the Protestant churches of America to surrender, in favor of the state, the traditional claim of the Christian Church to control the formal education of Christian children. The Christian Church, as that broad term is used, comprises not only the numerous Protestant

---

[10] See, for example, Ray A. Billington, *The Protestant Crusade*, pp. 142 ff. (New York: The Macmillan Company, 1938) ; George H. Martin, *Evolution of the Massachusetts Public School System*, p. 230 (New York: D. Appleton and Company, 1894) ; Arthur J. Hall, *Religious Education in Public Schools*, p. 55 (Chicago: University of Chicago Press, 1914).

[11] Richard J. Gabel, *Public Funds for Church and Private Schools*, pp. 285 ff. Washington: Catholic University of America, 1937.

[12] Vivian T. Thayer, *Religion in Public Education*, p. 7 (New York: The Viking Press, 1947), expresses a common opinion in finding this opposition based on fear of Catholicism.

[13] Charles A. Beard and Mary Beard, *The Rise of American Civilization*, I, p. 811 (2 vols., New York: The Macmillan Company, 1933). Alvin W. Johnson and Frank H. Yost, *Separation of Church and State in the United States*, p. 29 (Minneapolis: University of Minnesota Press, 1948), come to the same conclusion in almost exactly the same words. See also Brubacher, *op. cit.*, p. 335; Alvin P. Stauffer, *Anti-Catholicism in American Politics, 1865-1900*, p. 62 (unpublished dissertation, Harvard University, 1933).

denominations, but the various branches of the Orthodox Church and the Roman Catholic Church. It may be illuminating to discover the reasons why a church decided to turn over the control of the formal elementary education of its children to the state and to surrender its claim to control popular education. It may be even more illuminating to discover whether, and why, a church came to the conclusion that the control of popular elementary education should be vested solely in the state.

The term Protestantism as generally used covers large numbers of disparate groups and individuals, among whom all shades of opinion may be found on any conceivable question. It is obviously impossible, as well as pointless, to study the opinions on the control of popular education of all these individuals and groups, nor would all these opinions be found to have exercised influence upon the abandonment of the control of elementary education by the American Protestant churches. A selection must be made. If the selection is to be representative, it must include churches from all the major branches of Protestantism.

Practically all the Protestant churches may be traced back to one or more of four original sources, which have frequently commingled in the course of the centuries. These four streams are Anglicanism, Calvinism, Lutheranism, and Evangelicalism. It would be well to take some samplings from each; and the church or churches chosen from each group should be selected on the basis of their importance, resulting from numbers and influence, in establishing the pattern of the Protestant stand on the control of popular elementary education.

Since Anglicanism is represented in the United States by only one major church, the Protestant Episcopal Church, obviously no choice need be made here.

The philosophy and policies of the American Lutheran synods on the question of popular elementary education have already been investigated in Walter H. Beck's *Lutheran Ele-*

mentary Schools in the United States. It would be futile to repeat his work.

It would be equally pointless to repeat the investigations of Lewis J. Sherrill's *Presbyterian Parochial Schools,* which studies the history of church-controlled primary education in the major Calvinist church of Scotch derivation. The Calvinism of English origin can best be studied in the Congregational Church. The continental strains can be studied in the Dutch Reformed Church and the German Reformed Church.

As has already been noted, the churches of the Evangelical group are the major denominations, at least from the point of church membership, in the United States. None of these churches has been, either in Europe or in America, an established church with a history of control over public education. When the drive for popular education brought up the question of the control of that education in nineteenth-century America, the Evangelical churches could not fall back on a well-established educational tradition; they had to take their stand in the very rush and hurry of events.

In the present work the term Evangelicalism is used in the commonly accepted sense; that is, it is applied to those denominations which in Europe would be called dissenting as against the established church; the sects as against the churches; the "church gathered" as against the "church given." It is the tradition, as old as Protestantism, which stresses emotionalism, religious feeling. In its primitive stages at least, Evangelicalism would agree with the definition of its most prominent theologian, Schleiermacher, that theology is thought about emotion. Its original appeal has always been to the disinherited, the poor, and the uneducated. It generally makes its appearance as a sect of the lower classes; very frequently it evolves into a church of the middle classes.

Even to list the multitudinous Evangelical sects in the United States would be a lengthy task. Particularly among the Evangelical denominations does Protestantism merit the term "fissiparous" that has been applied to it. Once more, a selection must be made.

The Society of Friends is, numerically speaking, a small group, but the Quakers have been influential beyond their numbers. It would be well to consider their stand on the question of the control of popular elementary education.

The majority of Evangelicals in the United States may be found under the general denominational categories of Methodist and Baptist. The congregational polity which is a hallmark of Evangelicalism makes the study of the history of the Baptists particularly difficult. The present investigation will attempt to discover the drift of opinion in possibly the most influential of the loose Baptist groupings, the northern Baptists, now known as the American Baptist Convention. Fortunately, the Methodist Episcopal Church, the largest and most important group in nineteenth-century Methodism, provides an exception to the rule of congregational polity. The educational philosophy and policies of this church, now known as the Methodist Church, will be considered.

The present study will survey the thought of the chosen churches only on popular elementary education and that only within the United States. Most of these churches conduct elementary schools in their foreign missions. Many of them have select private schools for the children of their wealthier members. Many, during the nineteenth century, supported primary schools for the children of the poor, and conducted denominational secondary schools and colleges. These schools, however, are not efforts to implement the traditional claims of the Christian Church to control education. The problem is not to discover why the churches supplied elementary education to pagans or the poor or the wealthy; it is rather to find out why the churches gave up the control of the primary education of the children of their own membership.

The thought of the Protestant churches, or what might be called their educational philosophy so far as the control of education is concerned, obviously finds its most authoritative expression in the recommendations and resolutions of national conventions and congresses. Another very important source of information, which gives us, not only the final decisions reached, but also the antecedent thought leading to these decisions, is to be found in the various periodicals accepted as official or unofficial organs by the church in question. The present study will make the fullest possible use of both these sources.[14]

The terminal point of the present study will have been reached when American Protestantism, by and large, shall have withdrawn from the control of popular primary education, when the Protestant churches shall have relinquished, in favor of the state, the claim of the Christian Church to control the formal elementary education of Christian children.

---

[14] In the selection of these magazines large reliance has been placed on Frank L. Mott, editor, *History of American Magazines, 1741-1850* (New York: D. Appleton-Century Company, 1930). Also consulted were Peter G. Mode, *Source Book and Bibliographical Guide for American Church History* (Menasha: Banta Publishing Company, 1921), and denominational histories.

CHAPTER II

The Episcopalians

The Established Church of England has, possibly more than any other Protestant church in Europe, maintained a continuing interest in the field of education. With the first permanent English settlement in Virginia the traditions of the Anglican Church were transported to our shores. Consequently it would have been strange had the colonial branch of the Church of England not manifested an interest in education. It was instrumental in the establishment of one of our earliest colleges;[1] it conducted a number of lower schools;[2] it showed some concern for the education of the Negro slaves and the Indian aborigines.[3]

After the establishment of the United States the legitimate heir of the Anglican educational tradition was the Protestant Episcopal Church. Yet while the parent church had, by the middle of the nineteenth century, created over 8,500 elementary

---

[1] Donald G. Tewksbury, *The Founding of American Colleges and Universities before the Civil War*, p. 137 (New York: Teachers College, Columbia University, 1932) ; Sadie Bell, *The Church, the State, and Education in Virginia*, p. 114 (New York: Science Press, 1930).

[2] Clifton H. Brewer, *History of Religious Education in the Episcopal Church to 1835*, pp. 20-27. New Haven: Yale University Press, 1924.

[3] *Ibid.*, pp. 52 ff.

schools in Great Britain,[4] the Anglicans in America had founded only a handful.[5]

Although the Protestant Episcopal Church had been organized in 1785, the question of education was not discussed in the meetings of the triennial General Convention, the supreme governing body of the church, before the year 1811, when the Convention went on record as approving an Episcopalian secondary school.[6] In the subsequent meetings of the Convention there were discussions of various types of education—secondary schooling,[7] the training of Indians and Negroes,[8] charity schools.[9] The question of popular elementary education, however, was not introduced until 1838.

In that year a correspondent drew the attention of the *Churchman*, long the most influential of the Episcopalian weeklies, to the report of Calvin Stowe on popular primary education in Europe.[10] The editors decided that the matter was worth fol-

---

[4] Cubberley, *History of Education*, p. 632.

[5] Brewer, *op. cit.*, pp. 103 ff.; William W. Manross, *The Episcopal Church in the United States, 1800-1840*, pp. 76, 146 (New York: Columbia University Press, 1938).

  That the question of popular primary education never became of major interest to the Episcopal Church would seem to be indicated by the fact that none of the common histories here listed discusses the topic. See Edward C. Chorley, *Men and Movements in the American Episcopal Church* (New York: Charles Scribner's Sons, 1946); William W. Manross, *History of the American Episcopal Church* (Milwaukee: Morehouse Publishing Company, 1935); S. D. McConnell, *History of the American Episcopal Church* (Milwaukee: Young Churchman Company, 1916); William S. Perry, *History of the American Episcopal Church, 1587-1883* (2 vols., Boston: Osgood, 1885); Charles C. Tiffany, *History of the Protestant Episcopal Church* (New York: Charles Scribner's Sons, 1903); Samuel Wilberforce, *History of the Protestant Episcopal Church*, second edition (London: Rivington and Company, 1846).

[6] William S. Perry, editor, *Journals of the General Convention of the Protestant Episcopal Church, 1785-1835*, I, pp. 381-89. 3 vols., Claremont: Claremont Manufacturing Company, 1874.

[7] *Ibid.*, I, p. 523; II, pp. 29, 33, 59, 121, 138, 176, 193, 595.

[8] *Ibid.*, I, p. 468; II, p. 45.

[9] *Ibid.*, II, pp. 33, 145, 154, 259, 266, 391.

[10] *Churchman*, March 10, 1838.

lowing up, for in subsequent issues the *Churchman* printed extensive excerpts from Stowe's report.[11]

That the *Churchman's* discussion of popular education showed a good sense of timing is manifest by events that occurred during the General Convention of 1838. Apparently a good many Episcopalians were seriously disturbed by conditions in the common schools. This discontent brought quick action the day after the convention was called to order. A joint committee of the House of Bishops and of the House of Clerical and Lay Delegates was created to "consider the expediency of the adoption of measures by this convention, to provide more effectually for education, in conformity with the principles of the Protestant Episcopal Church."[12]

Before the committee reported, however, a meeting of both houses was held, outside the appointed sessions of the convention, to discuss the problem of popular education.[13] The speakers at this "informal committee of the whole"[14] dilated upon the evils growing out of the separation of learning from religion. They declared that the church should not only keep a watchful eye on the education provided in the common schools of the state, but that the church itself should set about the creation of a complete system of schools, for the support of which it had ample means.[15] One of the participating bishops later reported that

> it was agreed that the Church should take as much as was practicable of the education of the country on itself, particularly of those professing its faith. The Convention arrived at this conclusion from the great influence of the Church of Rome in America. Education was the right arm of her strength, and monasteries daily increased.[16]

---

[11] *Ibid.*, April 7, April 28, 1838.
[12] *Journal of General Convention, 1838*, pp. 18, 90.
[13] *Ibid.*, pp. 70, 107.
[14] *Journal of Christian Education*, I (1839), p. 2.
[15] *Churchman*, October 6, 1838.
[16] *Ibid.*, May 18, 1839.

Another episcopal report declared:

> That it was the duty of the Church to provide her own institutions for the Christian education of her children—not of her candidates for the ministry only, but of all within her pale—was a sentiment which was expressed with a degree of unanimity and feeling seldom witnessed within my experience on any other question.[17]

The meeting adopted resolutions which asserted that instruction in the Christian religion was necessary for all true education, called for the training of Christian teachers, declared it to be the duty of Episcopalians to maintain church schools, and insisted that these schools be established immediately.[18] Obviously, the Episcopalians still remembered the Anglican tradition of church control of education.

The General Convention, however, did not formally subscribe to the acts of the informal meeting. It was content to adopt the suggestion of its Joint Committee on Education that a continuing committee be set up to study the problems of education and report its findings to the next meeting of the General Convention.[19] The chief legislative body of the Episcopal Church was not to be stampeded into action.

The interest in general education bore quick fruit in the establishment of a magazine with the sesquipedalian title of *Journal of Christian Education and Family and Sunday School Visiter* [sic]. This periodical, designed as a monthly, issued but twelve numbers in the years 1839 and 1840, and ten in 1841; it achieved twelve issues only in 1842. With the death in that year of its chief editor, the Reverend Benjamin O. Peers, the journal ceased publication.

Its initial issue lauded the interest in education beginning to appear in the Episcopal Church. It found this interest the

---

[17] *Journal of Christian Education*, I (1839), p. 41.
[18] *Churchman*, October 6, 1838.
[19] *Journal of General Convention, 1838*, pp. 85, 123.

more necessary, since it discovered that the common schools of the state were of very questionable value.

> To speak in the most moderate terms upon the subject, it is now generally conceded that the morals of children are not *improved* by their attendance at school. Indeed, were we to reason exclusively from educational statistics, we should be driven to the conclusion that education is favorable to vice.[20]

The first editorial insisted on the obligations of both parents and minister to provide dogmatic instruction for the children of Episcopalians.

In subsequent issues of the magazine the editors continued to insist on the necessity of religion in education.[21] They found it a strange anomaly that, while religious instruction was offered in American colleges with but 6,000 students, no dogmatic teaching was given to the millions of pupils in the common schools.[22]

Strangely, the *Journal of Christian Education* did not, at first, mention parochial schools. This topic was first introduced in the November 1839 issue. The magazine declared that this was "a subject of no ordinary importance to the best interests of our beloved Church and country";[23] and it announced that its policy would be to work for the establishment of parochial schools in all parishes capable of sustaining them. In its subsequent issue the journal ran another editorial on parochial schools, contending that most Episcopalian parishes could afford to support one.[24] It buttressed its contention with a letter which noted that Catholics managed to support parish schools and urged Episcopalians to follow their example.[25]

---

20 *Journal of Christian Education*, I (1839), p. 1.
21 *Ibid.*, pp. 33-37, 40-42, 65-70.
22 *Ibid.*, p. 68.
23 *Ibid.*, p. 330.
24 *Ibid.*, pp. 361-64.
25 *Ibid.*, p. 365. Emulation of the Catholics was also urged in the *Churchman*, November 30, 1839.

A few months later the magazine made a harsh attack on the common schools.

> If it be true that in a majority of the schools a child is subjected to the contaminating influence of corrupt associates, without the security afforded by the counsel, checks, example and authority of a truly pious master; if ministers, parents, and Sunday School teachers find their most formidable opposition to arise from the counteracting effects of attendance upon the week-day school; if it be a fact, not to be disputed, that in the generality of cases it is not safe for a pious father to send his child to school, that he cannot have his intellect instructed, without putting in jeopardy the welfare of his soul—our only wonder is that this subject has not, long since, and universally, been acted upon as well as thought about, so that every parish of any strength should exhibit the beautiful spectacle of a church and schoolhouse side by side, in heavenly alliance, as if to bring up our children, literally as well as figuratively, under the droppings of the sanctuary.[26]

The periodical went on to declare that the only formidable obstacle to the establishment of a system of parochial schools was the lack of Episcopalian teachers. It promised that a future article would deal with the matter; "and the sum of our reply will be—the Church must *educate* them,—the Church *must* educate them,—*the Church* must educate them."[27]

Apparently the strictures on the common schools stirred some protests, for the *Journal of Christian Education* modified slightly the wholesale condemnation of the schools of the state. "We are not condemning in the mass all other schools; nor are we saying that the education therein received is worthless"; but we do insist that parochial schools are indispensable.[28] On this latter point the periodical insisted, even typographically. "We have no expectation of seeing the youth of the Church properly

---

[26] *Journal of Christian Education*, II (1840), p. 60.
[27] *Ibid.*, p. 62.
[28] *Ibid.*, p. 162.

educated, until we have, throughout the length and breadth of the land, PAROCHIAL SCHOOLS under the immediate supervision of the pastors of each congregation."[29]

In a convention called to consider ways and means to assist Episcopalian missions on the frontier, the question of popular primary education came up. The bishop in charge of the frontier warned that Catholics were making tremendous strides in the West, and demanded to know whether Episcopalians would tamely allow "their errors and superstitions to pervade the bosoms of tens of thousands who now reside there, and of the vast millions who at a future day will inhabit that most splendid and attractive country."[30] The bishop declared that the main source of danger was the schools which the Catholics, at great labor and expense, were founding in the West. He stated that the Catholic efforts for education

> demand our admiration, not our censure. But should they not call forth our most strenuous exertion to exhibit the Church in its true primitive and scriptural model, disenthralled from those human corruptions which have proved and may again prove subversive to civil liberty, and which may expose the followers of Christ to the imminent hazard and fearful reproach of superstition and idolatry.[31]

Another speaker declared that the union of religion and education was one of the principles of primitive Christianity. He found that Protestantism, as a whole, had failed in its duty toward education; particularly noteworthy was the dereliction of "our own church, in our own country."[32] He declared that the general Protestant opinion in the United States was that all connection between the church and education was "a matter

[29] *Ibid.*, p. 161.
[30] *Ibid.*, p. 235.
[31] *Ibid.*, p. 236.
[32] *Ibid.*, p. 238.

voluntary, accidental, and arbitrary—the open question of un-
restrained choice."[33] He refused to accept the divorce of the
church from education as an essential principle of Protestantism. Even though Protestantism had fallen away from the high
and true principles of the union of church and education, still
"among Protestant states our country alone acts openly on such
neglect."[34] That neglect the speaker would have amended.

To this unanimous chorus favoring ecclesiastical control of
popular education the *Journal of Christian Education* was glad
to add the voice of a bishop calling upon his diocese to establish
parochial schools.[35] The first voice *extra chorum* was that of the
bishop of Connecticut. While strongly recommending Episcopalian secondary schools, the bishop found that, since proselytizing
was rare in the common schools, parochial schools were super-
fluous, and the state schools were useful "in destroying party
and sectarian prejudices, and in promoting the general union
and common welfare."[36] A committee of the convention of the
diocese, while warning of the dangers of the public schools, expressed agreement with the bishop.[37] It urged that parents should
keep a careful eye on the common schools, and directed ministers to visit the schools and make their presence felt.

The clash of the Public School Society and Bishop Hughes
over the apportionment of funds for elementary schools in New
York City awoke echoes in the columns of the *Churchman.* The
first reaction of the weekly was to fall into line with the opponents of the Catholics.[38] It noted that the trustees of the Public
School Society claimed that their schools inculcated the Christian religion. The fact that the state approved the system of in-

---

[33] *Loc. cit.*
[34] *Ibid.,* p. 239.
[35] *Ibid.,* p. 216.
[36] *Ibid.,* p. 272.
[37] *Ibid.,* p. 312.
[38] *Churchman,* October 3, 1840.

struction of the Society "proves conclusively to our minds the establishment of the Christian religion by law."[39] Consequently the *Churchman* was of the opinion that the Catholic appeal should be rejected.

A few weeks later, however, the *Churchman* took sober second thought.[40] On examining the briefs of the society's lawyers, it found that they maintained that the state had the right to demand literacy, and to provide for it. With this the *Churchman* expressed agreement. It also concurred with the lawyers' contention that the state should provide moral education. But what, the *Churchman* asked itself, were the moral standards of the state? Were they Christian? The magazine had supposed that they were; but the law did not say so. The *Churchman* deliberated whether it was possible that Bishop Hughes was right. Obviously, a state system of education had many advantages, "though, as Churchmen, we are by no means prepared to recommend its adoption."[41] But if the state will not teach specifically Christian standards, the *Churchman* would like to see the school funds distributed "to the various denominations, Romanists, Protestants, Jews and Atheists."[42]

The *Journal of Christian Education* continued its campaign for parochial schools, and was happy to note that a number of such schools had been attempted.[43] It had also sorrowfully to note that practically all had been forced to close their doors, "and from a common cause, the *want of teachers*. The pupils have been promised, money has been furnished, rooms have been rented, but all to no purpose, *because instructors could not be found*."[44]

---

[39] *Loc. cit.*
[40] *Ibid.*, December 12, 1840.
[41] *Loc. cit.*
[42] *Loc. cit.*
[43] *Journal of Christian Education*, III (1841), 2.
[44] *Loc. cit.*

The journal viewed with interest the efforts of a royal commission to settle the problem of religion in the public schools of the Netherlands.[45] The commission found only two possible solutions. The first, to omit all religious instruction from the state schools, the journal declared "dreadful to our minds."[46] The magazine advocated the second plan, which envisioned parochial schools for both Protestants and Catholics.[47] ·

The efforts of the *Journal of Christian Education* to foster a demand for church primary schools did not achieve notable success. The interest in popular education manifested by the General Convention of 1838 had been dissipated when the convention reconvened in 1841. A number of dioceses reported actual or prospective secondary schools,[48] but no action was taken on the report of the Joint Committee on Education established by the Convention of 1838, save to refer it to the denominational Sunday School Union.[49] The convention commended education "to the various dioceses to take such order therein as the circumstances of the respective dioceses render expedient."[50] By this referral of the question to the local level the General Convention showed that the Episcopal Church was not ready or not willing to define a national policy on the question of popular education.

The failure of the General Convention to act, and the death of Peers and his *Journal of Christian Education*, apparently discouraged the proponents of parochial schools. For a number of years thereafter the Anglican periodicals did not touch upon the question. A correspondent of the *Churchman* urged that weekly

---

45 *Ibid.*, p. 199.
46 *Loc. cit.*
47 The efforts of the Church of England to set up primary church schools were also discussed. *Ibid.*, pp. 206-15, 241-43.
48 *Journal of General Convention, 1841*, pp. 40, 45, 55.
49 *Ibid.*, pp. 82, 133.
50 *Ibid.*, p. 83.

to campaign for religious education,[51] and, approving state support for Catholic parochial schools, requested Episcopalians to "emancipate the children of our poorer members from the control of a system [of common schools] so utterly subversive to right principle, as is the domination of this vile negation of all religion."[52]

Nor were the bishops completely silent. One asserted that every rector should have a school attached to his church,[53] and another averred that education could not but fail, until it was made the business of the Church.[54]

The columns of the *Churchman* were, for the remaining years of the forties, silent on the question of education under church control, save for a few letters advocating it in 1847.[55] The weekly broke its silence momentarily in 1851, when it published an excerpt from a statement by Archbishop Hughes reiterating the position of the Catholic Church. The editorial introduction of the statement indicates that the *Churchman* has resignedly accepted a *fait accompli*.

> Where was the harm of allowing each division of the great mass in this country, "calling themselves Christian," to establish and maintain and govern its own schools? . . . The old law distributing the school money among *all* free schools in proportion to the numbers of the scholars was just in principle, and if defective in execution and liable to abuse, it was not difficult to find and apply the remedy.[56]

The meetings of the General Convention continued their refusal to enact a general policy on popular primary education

---

[51] *Churchman*, January 22, 1842.

[52] *Ibid.*, January 29, 1842.

[53] *Journal of Christian Education*, IV (1842), p. 152.

[54] *Churchman*, October 8, 1842.

[55] *Ibid.*, July 31, August 7, August 21, 1847.

[56] *Ibid.*, December 6, 1851. See Chapter VI for the Methodist reaction to this issue of the *Churchman*.

for the Episcopal Church, but on the diocesan level some action was taken. While a number of dioceses reported their efforts for secondary education to the General Convention of 1844,[57] the dioceses of Maryland and South Carolina announced the existence within their borders of parochial schools.[58] At the General Convention of 1847 Florida, Louisiana, and Missouri were added to the number of dioceses reporting such schools.[59] By the time of the meeting of the General Convention of 1850, Tennessee and North Carolina had joined the group.[60]

The dioceses reporting parochial schools were in southern states. Precisely in those states public-school systems were not in successful operation until after the Civil War. It would appear that the drive for Episcopalian parish schools was most effective in those sections where the common schools had not as yet taken root.

In the General Convention of 1850 the first move in the direction of the establishment of the present Episcopalian religious orders was taken. (The term "religious order" was not, of course, used.) One of the motives behind this action was specifically "the education of the young."[61] The committee of bishops set up by the Convention of 1850 to discuss the problem reported in 1853 that they had not devised an acceptable plan.[62] The actual foundation of the religious orders was therefore postponed until after the Civil War.

The major Episcopalian quarterlies showed a disinclination to discuss popular elementary education. The *Protestant Episcopal Quarterly*, for example, which was born in 1854 and died after a short life of seven years, never touched upon the ques-

---

[57] *Journal of General Convention, 1844*, pp. 195-205.
[58] *Ibid.*, pp. 201, 204.
[59] *Ibid., 1847*, pp. 187, 189, 195.
[60] *Ibid., 1850*, pp. 167, 175.
[61] *Ibid.*, p. 132.
[62] *Ibid., 1853*, p. 188.

tion. It was not until 1854 that the *Church Review* got round
to the topic.

In that year the *Church Review* published an article discussing the neglect of Christian training.[63] The writer said that he
would not think of attacking the schools of the state. He declared
that "no one will maintain that our Common Schools are directly
injurious to morals."[64] But, he went on, juxtaposing two asser-
tions as premises from which the reader is to draw an obvious
conclusion, "first, our Common Schools have become almost
wholly secular," and "secondly, there has been an alarming increase of crime."[65]

The article went on to blame the expulsion of religious instruction from the public schools on what it termed the "revival
system," the Evangelical Protestant doctrine of "conversion."[66]
Summarily, this doctrine taught that men became Christians
through an emotional upheaval, caused by the action of the
Holy Ghost, in which sinners took Jesus as their Savior. This
theory of the instantaneous mutation of men had, the writer
found, brought into contempt "all the ordinary means of influence, and all the ordinary exhibitions of moral and religious
character."[67] Until Americans generally agreed that Christian
character was developed by training, and not instantaneously
created by "conversion," there was little hope of improvement
in the state schools. Dogmatic instruction must be reintroduced
into the common schools; if it is not, "we confess we see no
remedy but parochial or Church schools."[68]

---

[63] *Church Review*, VII (1854-1855), pp. 86-97. This periodical, later renamed the
American Quarterly Church Review and Ecclesiastical Register, will be cited
under its original title.

[64] *Ibid.*, p. 89.

[65] *Loc. cit.*

[66] For further details of this "conversion" see the author's *Major Trends in American Church History*, pp. 10-12 (New York: America Press, 1946).

[67] *Church Review, vol. cit.*, p. 91.

[68] *Ibid.*, p. 95.

The Know-Nothing excitement of the early fifties modified the viewpoint of a great many Protestant magazines. The *Church Review* did not escape the anti-Catholic contagion. In common with the nativist magazines of the time, it discovered

> simultaneous and adroitly planned efforts put forth in all parts of the country, on the part of the Romish priesthood, either to banish the Bible from our Public Schools, so as to make them absolutely atheistic in character, or else to break down the whole Common School System altogether.[69]

The quarterly, so recently critical of the public schools, now discovered that the state school system was the most efficient instrument to create a "true American nationality of character."[70]

In a later article the *Church Review* asserted that it would not condemn the public schools as wholly imperfect, or accuse them of being "godless."[71] But while the state schools could not be excused of the charge of fostering indifference and the neglect of religion,[72] the writer urged his fellow Episcopalians, for the sake of their young, to do their best to extend and strengthen the work of church schools.[73]

That some Anglicans were doing just that is indicated by the reports to the General Convention of 1856. Three dioceses, Kentucky, Wisconsin, and Western New York, joined the growing list of ecclesiastical provinces maintaining elementary schools.[74] New Jersey and Georgia reported to the General Convention of 1859 that they, too, had parochial schools.[75]

At the latter convention a Committee of the Laity was established to consider ways and means to assist the work of the

---

[69] *Ibid.*, VIII (1855-1856), p. 23.
[70] *Loc. cit.*
[71] *Ibid.*, XII (1859-1860), p. 67.
[72] *Ibid.*, pp. 68-71.
[73] *Ibid.*, pp. 75-82.
[74] *Journal of General Convention, 1856*, pp. 231, 248, 256.
[75] *Ibid., 1859*, pp. 254, 277.

church.[76] Before the convention adjourned *sine die,* the question
of popular education under church control was added to the
agenda of the committee.[77]

The report of this committee was published before the next
meeting of the General Convention. It declared it to be the spirit
and intention of the Episcopal Church to take full charge of the
education of its younger members.[78] The committee asserted
that it knew "of no more effective mode than the establishment
of parish schools wherever practicable."[79] It made it clear that
these parochial schools should not be charity schools. "We do
not mean schools for the poor only, but schools which shall be
equal to the best, where all the children of the parish shall be
educated under like influences."[80]

This call to action, made by a committee of its own creation,
could scarcely be ignored by the General Convention. At the
triennial meeting of 1862 the Committee on the State of the
Church brought in a special report on education.[81] The report
noted the increased attention paid to popular education, and
urged the convention to encourage it. It stressed the necessity of
increasing "the means of Christian education, by establishing
parochial schools, as far as practicable, in all our parishes."[82]

With the Civil War then in progress, the southern dioceses
of the church had withdrawn from the General Convention.
Consequently only a few dioceses reported parochial schools:
Maryland had 20 with 1,008 pupils, Minnesota 7 with 375 students, and New Jersey 19 with 679 scholars.[83]

---

[76] *Ibid.,* p. 124.
[77] *Ibid.,* p. 139.
[78] *Address of the Committee of the Laity,* p. 18. New York: The Committee, 1860.
[79] *Ibid.,* p. 19.
[80] *Loc. cit.*
[81] *Journal of General Convention, 1862,* pp. 65-66.
[82] *Ibid.,* p. 65.
[83] *Ibid.,* pp. 184, 190, 199.

When the subsequent General Convention was called to order, the new Standing Committee on Christian Education presented its initial report.[84] Its first proposal was to jettison the ideal of a parochial school beside every church. While approving the concern of well-to-do church members in sending their children to private church schools, the report found that the church had to provide for poorer Episcopalians. It asserted, however, that in providing this aid the church

> must not come in conflict with the State, nor need she do it. In some dioceses, the public schools are so admirable in every respect but the one, that we could not expect without the most lavish expenditure to compete with them, even if we were able to offer the education gratuitously.
>
> All that can be urged upon the whole Church is that her ministers and people will not simply acquiesce in whatever schools may happen to be near them, but conscientiously do their best to provide *Christian* education for the children of the Church.[85]

As to the means of conveying this Christian education, the committee offered several suggestions: parochial schools, church infant schools, "released-time" instruction, the exertion of Episcopalian influence on the public schools.

At the General Convention of 1868 the Standing Committee on Christian Education declared that it had nothing to add to the report of 1865.[86] It asserted its belief that in Episcopalian education "the condition of things is very deplorable."[87] The committee offered a novel definition of the term "parochial school." "By Parochial schools we mean those parish schools where free education is given to the children of the poorer classes."[88] These parochial schools should be distinguished from

---

[84] *Ibid., 1865*, pp. 372-80.
[85] *Ibid.,* p. 375.
[86] *Ibid., 1868*, p. 439.
[87] *Ibid.,* p. 440.
[88] *Ibid.,* p. 442.

the grammar schools, which the committee believed to be "just now the most practical and efficient shape which Christian education can take."[89] Grammar schools, which were to be supported by tuition, should be set up in all the larger towns and cities. The committee pointed out the greatest obstacle to the establishment of these schools. "It may be easy to found the schools; but whence are the teachers to come?"[90] The only plan that the committee could suggest was the creation of religious orders dedicated to the work of education.

At this convention the House of Bishops created its own Standing Committee on Christian Education.[91] This new committee brought in its first report before the convention adjourned. It asserted the need of Episcopalian schools "at a cost not so far exceeding the charges of some schools in which corrupt religion prevails."[92] To supply the necessary teachers, the report urged the formation of religious orders. The Catholic term "religious orders," however, was not used. The proposed groups were labeled "associations."[93]

In the interim before the next General Convention the Episcopalian periodicals had little to say on the subject of popular elementary education. The *Churchman*, however, did publish a few articles on the topic, and gave its blessing to efforts to sustain church schools.[94]

In the General Convention of 1870 the Standing Committees on Christian Education of both houses, united in a joint committee, issued a common report.[95] While praising parochial

---

[89] *Loc. cit.*
[90] *Loc. cit.*
[91] *Ibid.*, p. 187.
[92] *Ibid.*, p. 219. "Corrupt religion" or "corrupt Christianity" was a common circumlocution for Catholicism.
[93] *Loc. cit.*
[94] *Churchman*, January 16, November 13, 1869; August 26, 1871.
[95] *Journal of General Convention, 1871*, pp. 586-89.

schools, it considered them merely auxiliaries to the public
school system.

> And where they are practicable, and can be rendered efficient, espe-
> cially in those parts of the country where common schools are
> deficient in number or thoroughness of training, they should be
> heartily sustained. But they can only in a very limited degree
> supply the place of the public schools of the country.[96]

The committee declared that the Episcopal Church should extend
cordial support to the schools of the state "from the inspiration
of patriotism" and "for the sake of Christianity itself."[97] Having
imparted its blessing to state control of popular primary education, the convention adjourned.

The original *Churchman* had suspended publication in the
early days of the Civil War. When, after peace had been
achieved, a second *Churchman* made its appearance, it continued the traditional policy of its predecessor in support of
church schools,[98] but a note of hostility to the Catholic educational position was sounded.[99]

In the General Convention of 1874 no notable developments
were reported by the Joint Committee on Christian Education.
Its report stressed the need of Episcopalian teachers and again
suggested the establishment of teaching religious orders.[100]
Approximately 165 parochial schools with 7,500 pupils were
reported to the convention.[101]

The fear of the alleged Catholic threat to the state schools
now infected the *Churchman*. In the course of a series of articles

---

[96] *Ibid.,* p. 586.

[97] *Ibid.,* p. 587.

[98] *Churchman,* September 7, 1872; September 20, 1873; September 5, September
19, 1874.

[99] *Ibid.,* September 20, 1873.

[100] *Journal of General Convention, 1874,* pp. 536-39.

[101] *Ibid.,* p. 540. The *Journal of General Convention, 1880,* p. 365, claims 2,500
teachers and 36,953 pupils in 1874.

it radically changed its stand on the control of education.[102]
Finally it declared:

> It is necessary in *our* government,—in fact, in *any* government,—to
> have instruction given to children which will tend to sustain and
> strengthen government; and we Americans calculate to give this
> instruction in schools over which the government shall have com-
> plete control.
>
> Let the Roman Catholic have his own school, if he will, and
> withal be exempted from taxation for the schools sanctioned by the
> State; but let the inevitable result be, loss of all qualifications as
> a voter.[103]

Thus anti-Catholic animus changed the strongest champion of
church-controlled popular education into a proponent of state
control of education.

At the Second Church Congress of the Episcopal Church
other voices were raised to demand universal compulsory education in secularized public schools.[104] The church was told that
it conducted schools, not of right, but only on tolerance of the
state, which alone had the right to conduct schools.[105]

The Third Church Congress explicitly considered the question of religious and secular education. The first speech on the
topic, accepting state control of primary education, called upon
the Episcopal Church to exert its influence on the common
schools.[106] The second orator lamented the secularization of the
public schools, and urged their retention of the Bible.[107] The
third speaker, on the other hand, demanded the complete secu-

---

[102] *Churchman,* January 2, January 30, June 5, September 4, September 18, October 9, October 16, 1875.

[103] *Ibid.,* October 16, 1875.

[104] *Proceedings of the Second Church Congress,* pp. 24-30. New York: Thomas
Whittaker, 1876.

[105] *Ibid.,* p. 25.

[106] *Report of the Third Church Congress,* pp. 131 ff. New York: Thomas Whittaker,
1876.

[107] *Ibid.,* pp. 144 ff.

larization of public education.[108] The final address, while conceding the rights of the state in popular education, demanded that the control of that education be vested in the church.[109] Obviously the deliberations of the congress were inconclusive. It is clear, however, that the earlier Episcopalian unanimity on the control of education no longer existed.

The effects of that lost unanimity were shown in the General Convention of 1877. The report of the Joint Committee on Education was summed up in its concluding resolutions, which were adopted by the convention.

> It is the solemn conviction of the General Convention, in both Houses, that the Holy Bible should be retained in our common schools; and that it is the duty of the Clergy and the Laity of the Church to take, so far as the opportunity is offered them, an active interest in the education provided by the State, with the idea of infusing into it as much of religious influence and instruction as possible; to supplement it with religious instruction everywhere; and to add proper church schools for the whole work, wherever they are needed, and the means can be commanded for their support.[110]

In effect, the Episcopal Church rejected its educational heritage. The control of popular education was yielded to the state. The duty of the church to assume full control of the education of its young, once unanimously accepted, was denied.

Symptomatic of the new policy, the General Convention of 1880 supplanted the Joint Committee on Christian Education by a Committee on Education under the Auspices of the Protestant Episcopal Church.[111] The last report of the expiring com-

---

[108] *Ibid.*, pp. 146 ff.
[109] *Ibid.*, pp. 149 ff.
[110] *Journal of General Convention, 1877*, p. 521. Parochial schools with 9,365 pupils were reported; *ibid.*, p. 354.
    The *Churchman* occasionally mentioned the school question. See the issues for May 26, 1877; November 2, 1878; December 6, 1879.
[111] *Journal of General Convention, 1880*, p. 38.

mittee sounded a note of failure. "It seems not too much to say that very little of systematic effort has been produced by the reports of the Committee, or the deliberations of the General Convention."[112] It issued a last call to the church to "take the subject of education into her own hands; to surround and guard her children in *all* their training with the instructions and influence of religion, according to her own tenets and order."[113] In its view, Christian education was still only "education under the auspices and guardianship of the Protestant Episcopal Church."[114]

With the death of this committee expired the attempt to implement the Anglican idea of church control of elementary education. Although reports on parochial schools continued to be made, the General Convention no longer discussed the problem.[115]

The drive for Episcopalian parochial schools had lasted less than fifty years. It was not until the movement for popular elementary education had attained appreciable proportions that Episcopalians developed an interest in church schools. Two stimuli motivated their interest. Of lesser importance was emulation of schools conducted by the Catholic Church. Much more important was Episcopalian reaction to the schools of the state. Episcopalians considered the common schools to be, at best, deficient in an essential of education, religious training. While

---

[112] *Ibid.*, p. 436.
[113] *Ibid.*, p. 437.
[114] *Loc. cit.*
[115] The subject was mentioned in passing in 1895; *ibid., 1895*, p. 628.

    Reports on parochial schools, however, continued to be made. These reports included figures from foreign missions. They indicate a lack of growth of Episcopalian primary schools.

Year	Teachers	Pupils	Reference
1880	920	12,287	*Journal of General Convention, 1880*, p. 375
1883	804	10,488	*Ibid., 1883*, p. 482
1886	745	13,308	*Ibid., 1886*, p. 593
1889	586	10,281	*Ibid., 1889*, p. 559
1892	433	10,246	*Ibid., 1892*, p. 461
1895	490	11,541	*Ibid., 1895*, p. 436

it did not deny the right of the state to conduct schools, the Episcopal Church would not place the stamp of approval on them.

Although the principle of a complete system of education under the sole control of the Episcopal Church was enunciated, the denomination took no steps, as a national organization, to implement it. Locally, a number of dioceses, chiefly in the South, managed to set up parochial schools before the Civil War. The church drive for schools succeeded only where the state had not yet established common schools.

At the time of the Civil War the call for a parochial school beside each church sounded with renewed vigor in Episcopalian organs of opinion. But soon the call was significantly modified to a demand for parochial schools "wherever practicable." It was agreed that the church school was no longer practicable where the state school system was firmly planted.

With the acceptance of the public schools came a modification of the Episcopalian viewpoint regarding them. Although they continued to be censured for their neglect of religious training, they were no longer stigmatized as schools of vice. The Episcopal Church abandoned its former policy of abstention, and began to urge its members to exert Episcopalian influence on the common schools. Indeed, the General Convention reached the point where it officially endorsed the state schools "for the sake of Christianity itself."

The movement for Episcopalian parochial schools was largely spent before 1880. Some irreconcilables still raised their voices in defense of the defeated ideal of church-controlled primary education. Others, motivated largely by animus against Catholicism, called for a completely secularized elementary education under the sole control of the state. The Episcopal Church did not formally reject the claim of the Christian Church to control popular elementary education; but to the voices upholding the sole right of the state to control that education, it answered with the silence of consent.

CHAPTER III

The Congregationalists

Since the educational endeavors of the colonial Puritans have been recounted in every general history of American education, there is no need to rehearse that story here.[1] Nor is there need to decide whether the schools of the Puritan colony were the foundation of the present system of public schools. Cubberley declares that they were;[2] Knight and the Beards insist they were not.[3] Nor need an opinion be expressed whether education in colonial New England was a function of the state rather than of the church. Greene holds that it was;[4] Knight maintains that it was not.[5] There is, however, general agreement that the main motive in the establishment and conduct of the early New England schools was religious.

When speaking of colonial days the historians of Congregationalism stress the interest of Puritan leaders in education

---

[1] E.g., Cubberley, *Public Education in the United States,* pp. 20 ff.; Monroe, *op. cit.,* pp. 105 ff.; Knight, *op. cit.,* pp. 97 ff.

[2] Cubberley, *Public Education in the United States,* p. 25; and his *History of Education,* p. 366.

[3] Knight, *op. cit.,* p. 105; Beard and Beard, *op. cit.,* I, p. 177.

[4] Evarts B. Greene, *Religion and the State,* p. 120. New York: New York University Press, 1941.

[5] Knight, *op. cit.,* pp. 98, 106.

and claim for the church of the English Calvinists the authorship of the free public-school systems of the present day.[6] None of these general histories, however, discuss the relation of the Congregational Church to the drive for popular primary education in the first half of the nineteenth century. It would appear that that movement received little impetus from the Puritan Church.

The Congregationalists remained largely true to the polity expressed in their denominational name. Although they established various local associations, they did not establish their National Council until after the Civil War. Before that event, the most influential of the local groupings was the General Association of Massachusetts in the very center of the Puritan stronghold of New England.

At the annual meetings of this General Association between the years 1809 and 1848, only once was the topic of popular elementary education introduced. In 1835 this assemblage created a committee to discuss education in the distant territory of Indiana. Following its report, the Association voiced its opinion that the United States needed vigorous and perservering efforts in behalf of elementary education, and especially in the growing West, "that very interesting and important portion of our country."[7]

More interest was shown in the problem in the forties by two influential Congregationalist quarterlies which were founded in that decade, the *New Englander* at Yale and the *Bibliotheca Sacra* at Harvard. The New Haven periodical was the first to touch upon the question. Condemning Protestants who sent their

---

[6] Gaius G. Atkins and Frederick L. Fagley, *History of American Congregationalism,* pp. 229 ff. (Boston: Pilgrim Press, 1942) ; Albert E. Dunning, *The Congregationalists in America,* p. 363 (Boston: Pilgrim Press, 1894) ; Williston Walker, *A History of the Congregational Churches in the United States,* p. 151 (New York: Charles Scribner's Sons, 1900) ; Sanford Fleming, *Children and Puritanism,* p. 104 (New Haven: Yale University Press, 1933).

[7] *Minutes of the General Association of Massachusetts, 1835,* p. 9.

children to Catholic schools, the magazine discussed the proper method of treating Catholics with respect to the state schools.[8] It noted that the Catholic Church had a large membership of recent immigrants, who were not highly regarded in the Yale halls. "As foreigners and as Roman Catholics, they are incomparably the most ignorant class of our population."[9] The *New Englander* expressed the opinion that the Catholic Church could keep its membership in the United States only as long as that membership was kept in ignorance. Consequently it demanded that the children of Catholics be educated in the state schools, even though, in order to induce them to enter, the Bible had to be sacrificed. "It is better that Roman Catholic children should be educated in public schools in which the Bible is not read, than that they should be not educated at all, or educated in schools under the absolute control of their priesthood."[10] Thus in its earliest days did an influential Congregationalist publication not only accept the thesis that the control of popular elementary education belonged to the state, but expressed its disapproval of the efforts of a Christian church to keep that education in its own hands.

Again in 1846 the *New Englander*, discussing common schools, took for granted state control of primary education.[11] While most denominational magazines of the day would have lamented the lack of religious instruction as the most serious shortcoming of the state schools, the Yale quarterly found their gravest defect to be the lack of division of the pupils into grades.[12] When in 1847 Horace Mann was concluding his long period of service as secretary of the Massachusetts Board of

---

[8] *New Englander,* II (1844), p. 235.
[9] *Ibid.,* p. 240.
[10] *Loc. cit.*
[11] *Ibid.,* IV (1846), pp. 522-31.
[12] *Ibid.,* p. 528.

Education in controversy, the *New Englander* supported the doughty champion of the common schools.[13]

While the *New Englander* was proclaiming its faith in the state schools, doubts began to assail the minds of many Congregationalists. In 1848 the General Association of Massachusetts established a committee with orders to report the following year on the suitableness of the common schools for the children of Congregationalists. At the meeting of 1849 the report of the committee was adopted and printed in the minutes.[14]

The committee paid due honor to the theory that religious instruction was necessary to education. Admitting that in this matter the common schools fell short of perfection, the committee expressed its belief that the matter could scarcely be remedied. If universal elementary education was to be achieved, the intervention of the state was necessary. The numerous sects of Christianity made it impossible for the state schools to provide religious instruction to the satisfaction of all. Still, the benefits of the state system of schools were so great that the lack of instruction in Congregationalist dogma, which could be otherwise supplied, was not a sufficient reason for the Puritan congregations to withdraw their children.

If, however, the Association wanted another system of education, the committee recommended, not parochial schools, but "private schools formed by the union of Evangelical Christians of different denominations, in which all the fundamental doctrines of Christianity could be taught."[15] It would be a "great evil,"[16] the committee declared, to withdraw the influence and presence of Congregationalists from the state schools. For the present the church should keep an eye on the common schools

---

13 *Ibid.*, V (1847), pp. 513-22.
14 *Minutes of the General Association of Massachusetts, 1849*, pp. 8-10.
15 *Ibid.*, p. 10.
16 *Loc. cit.*

and try to improve them. It should not create private schools unless the condition in the public schools clearly required such radical action.

The committee ended by approving universal primary education, lauding the "enlarged and benevolent views of our Puritan ancestors in establishing our present system of free schools," and urging Congregationalists to support and improve the schools of the state.[17]

With the adoption of this report by the General Association ended all efforts to reclaim for the Puritan Church the control of popular elementary education. Not only did the Congregationalist Church agree that the state should control popular education, but it held that its own branch of the Christian Church should not venture into that field. The Puritan Church had indeed evolved since the days of the Cottons and the Mathers.

While the committee of the General Association was composing its report, the *New Englander* was investigating the relation of education to the well-being of states.[18] It took pride in the fact that "the first system of free schools in the history of our race was adopted on these western shores,"[19] and attributed the prosperity of the northern states to that happy fact. It was positive that a generation of universal education, while making the nation still more prosperous, healthy, and happy, would also wipe out 90 per cent of all crime and poverty. "We owe our salvation to our public schools."[20]

In the same volume of the *New Englander* the Reverend S. W. S. Dutton discussed "The Proposed Substitution of Sectarian for Public Schools."[21] Besides the Catholics and some Episco-

---

[17] *Loc. cit.*
[18] *New Englander*, VI (1848), pp. 207-19.
[19] *Ibid.*, p. 208.
[20] *Ibid.*, p. 213.
[21] *Ibid.*, pp. 230-49.

palians, the author found among the enemies of the common school the old-school Presbyterians. These latter, he feared, were communicating the infection to their fellow Calvinists, the Congregationalists. His article was designed to warn his coreligionists against the evils of church schools.

Dutton declared that the United States could not support two systems of schools. His considered opinion was that a system of church schools "would be a death-blow to the prosperity, and probably to the existence, of public schools."[22] While the state schools had had a history of two centuries of satisfactory service, the church school was an untried experiment. In the author's opinion it would be foolish to reject a tool of proven utility in order to make a costly test of an extremely doubtful instrument.

As to the right of the state to control popular elementary education, the author found no question; the matter "has not to our knowledge been raised in this country. That question could hardly be raised here. It would not find enough variety or diversity of opinion to secure its discussion."[23]

The author found that, while church schools would reach only part of the American children, the common schools were well designed to secure the rudimentary education of the whole people. All Americans, with the exception of some Catholics, were willing to trust their children to the state schools; and if a few changes were made, even the Catholics would come in.

The state schools, Dutton went on, cannot but impart an education superior to that of the church schools. The common schools are in accord with "the necessities and nature of our free institutions, with the comprehensive character of Christianity, and with the liberal spirit of the age."[24] On the other hand, church schools cannot but be "sectarian, divisive, narrow,

---

[22] *Ibid.*, p. 233.
[23] *Ibid.*, p. 235.
[24] *Ibid.*, p. 240.

clannish, anti-republican."[25] While the public schools produce good Americans, it can be questioned whether the parochial schools do the same.

Confident that his readers were convinced, Dutton examined the religious objection to the common schools. This objection, he maintained, could be met by placing all sects on an equal footing in the schools.

> The opposite principle, which has been so extensively adopted in the discussion of this subject, that in this country, the state or civil power is Christian and Protestant, and therefore that the schools sustained and directed in part thereby are Christian and Protestant, and that whoever attends them has no right to object to a rule requiring all to study Christian and Protestant books and doctrines, we wholly disbelieve and deny. The state, the civil power in whatever form in this country, is no more Protestant, or Christian, than it is Jewish or Mohammedan. It is of no religion whatever.[26]

Religious instruction is not the task of the state, but of the church. Dogmatic teaching is necessary for a well-rounded education; but "education in common schools is not, and is not designed to be, a *complete* education."[27] To round out common-school education, Dutton suggested the equivalent of present-day "released-time" practices, and declared that the state schools should be completely secularized.

The Congregational quarterlies were joined in 1849 by a weekly destined to become one of the most influential periodicals of the time. The *Independent* boasted as editors some of the most prominent Congregationalists of the nineteenth century. Until the Civil War the weekly was edited by Leonard Bacon, Richard Storrs, and Joseph P. Thompson, and during the sixties by Henry Ward Beecher and Theodore Tilton. Under

---

25 *Loc. cit.*
26 *Ibid.*, p. 242.
27 *Ibid.*, p. 243.

the guidance of Henry C. Bowen, which lasted until the end of the century, it at one time achieved a circulation of 100,000. Although under Tilton it had dropped "Congregationalists" from its masthead, it continued to speak for an influential segment of that church.

From its earliest days the *Independent* championed state-controlled education. It declared that the free-school law of New York was "worthy to be inscribed in columns of marble in every town of the State."[28]

> Let us by all means have free schools! and when they are once established, let all use their best endeavors to make the Common schools so excellent, that there shall be neither room nor occasion for private schools.[29]

The weekly viewed with equanimity the prospect of secularized education. "Surely it is better that the people should be taught to read and write without being taught at the same time the Assembly's Catechism or the Thirty Nine Articles, than that they should not be taught to read and write."[30]

The Congregationalist chorus lauding the public schools was joined by a new voice in 1851. The *Bibliotheca Sacra* published an article designed to prove that universal primary education should be provided by the state.[31] The article declared that universal education was "the readiest and surest road to public prosperity and wealth"[32] and even to longevity, for "there are certain elements in Christian knowledge and culture, the tendency of which is to prolong human existence."[33] State schools, the author urged, should teach Christian dogmatics, even if this

---

[28] *Independent*, April 5, 1849.
[29] *Ibid.*, November 1, 1849. See also the issues for December 13, 1849; June 20, 1850.
[30] *Ibid.*, November 28, 1850. See also January 30, 1851.
[31] *Bibliotheca Sacra*, VIII (1851), pp. 734-66.
[32] *Ibid.*, p. 746.
[33] *Ibid.*, p. 750.

meant sectarian teaching; for education without religion is "education without its essence."[34] And the article concluded with a fine flourish of rhodomontade.

> Let us do what in us lies, by our counsels, for example, and our votes, to stimulate and perfect the common school—the People's College, the great fountain of popular light, the mighty bulwark of constitutional liberty.[35]

Congregationalist disapproval of Presbyterian parochial schools, first expressed in the *New Englander*, was now seconded by the *Independent*. In 1849 the weekly was content merely to note the existence of the Presbyterian schools,[36] but in 1852 it leveled stringent criticism at the educational policy of the Scotch church. Using the device of identifying the common schools alone as American, it condemned the Presbyterian parochial schools.[37] It rejected the Presbyterian contention that education should be controlled by the church. While English Congregationalists could scarcely be damned for "un-Americanism," the *Independent* regretted their parochial schools. "We are ashamed to say that the Independents, or Congregationalists, in England, are, as a body, carried away with the same opinion."[38] It summed up the case of state-versus-church schools:

> This system secures an education to all the people, while that would leave a large part in entire ignorance. This system tends greatly to mitigate the asperities of sectarian feeling, and that would make them tenfold of what they are now. The present system is an important check against Romanism; that would contribute to the strength and progress of the Roman system.[39]

---

34 *Ibid.*, p. 762.
35 *Ibid.*, p. 766.
36 *Independent*, January 4, 1849.
37 *Ibid.*, August 19, 1852.
38 *Loc. cit.* The English Congregationalists had, by 1852, established over four hundred elementary schools; Cubberley, *History of Education*, p. 632.
39 *Independent, art. cit.*

Stirred to anger, the *Presbyterian* declared that "it is shameless in the Independent to make such a representation of the matter, by placing Presbyterians by the side of Roman Catholics in their opposition" to the schools of the state.[40] No one in the country considered the common schools more of a blessing than did Presbyterians.

Equally angry, the *Independent* put its case for common schools. Imperative necessity demanded them, due to the recent increase of infidelity and of "a Roman Catholic population, priest-ridden and bound in chains of hereditary ignorance."[41] Only a minority approved parochial schools—Catholics, Presbyterians, and a few Episcopalians whose parochial schools did not exist outside "the unfortunate little diocese" in which they had originated.[42] Nor could the Presbyterians deny that they opposed state control of education; to prove its point the *Independent* cited the Presbyterian Board of Education.

> "The direction of our schools would be religious instead of political, under the Church instead of the State. AND THIS IS THE TRUE PLAN." Will the Presbyterian please to say which side of the question about common schools is taken by the Board of Education?[43]

Temporarily, the *Independent* allowed the matter to rest. Congregationalists were more concerned about a national convention of their church, held in Albany in 1852. This meeting did not touch upon the question of popular education.[44] In 1853, however, the magazine found occasion to condemn Catholic parochial schools and to regret that Episcopalians and Presbyterians were following the bad example of the Catholics. It de-

---

[40] *Presbyterian*, September 2, 1852.
[41] *Independent*, September 18, 1852.
[42] *Loc. cit.*
[43] *Loc. cit.*
[44] *Proceedings of the General Convention of Congregational Ministers and Delegates.* New York: S. W. Benedict, 1852.

clared that it would be an evil day for the nation if the state schools were abandoned for "the narrow and petty system of parochial sectarian schools."[45] Later in the year it published the letter which Joseph Thompson, one of its editors, had sent to Richard Cobden in support of his demand for state elementary schools in England.[46] The letter declared that all American Christians, with the exception of the Catholics and some few Episcopalians and Presbyterians, gave enthusiastic support to the public schools, and found them no danger to the faith and morals of their children. Americans were agreed on a number of principles: the people must be educated; it is impossible to secure universal education save through the agency of the state; common schools should not teach Christian doctrine; Christians should support state education rather than private or parochial institutions of learning.

At the height of the Know-Nothing propaganda in the fifties, the *New Englander* was moved to investigate the alien Catholic threat to American liberties.[47] It found it noteworthy that "the Catholics are strongest where the Protestant place of worship and the Puritan schoolhouse are least known and felt—a fact suggestive of better means than proscriptive legislation to save our free institutions from the Pope of Rome."[48] The quarterly recounted the large sums spent by Massachusetts on its common schools, and attributed to the American dollar not omnipotence, but intelligence. "Against such an annual array of mental forces, directed mostly by the government of the commonwealth, what can the Jesuit or hostile foreigner do to the injury of the State?"[49] It praised the common schools for their power to

---

45 *Independent*, March 31, 1853.
46 *Ibid.*, November 17, 1853.
47 *New Englander*, XIII (1855), pp. 262-76.
48 *Ibid.*, p. 268.
49 *Ibid.*, p. 275.

render the children of immigrants "liberalized, Americanized, and with an import far beyond its technical, naturalized."[50]

That these schools of the state were compelled to retain the Bible was the contention of a Dutch Reformed pastor, the Reverend J. H. Seelye, in an article published in the *Bibliotheca Sacra*.[51] Declaring that a state must be based on a religion for its very existence, Seelye found the religion of the United States to be the Bible. "It is therefore the most vital demand upon the American State, that the Bible be taught in American schools."[52] Nor should the teaching of that religion be confined to the church; "it follows with unbending necessity that the State must teach its religion."[53] Seelye gave short shrift to objectors to this religion imposed and taught by the state. "If the will of the State come in conflict with the will or conscience of an individual, the individual may suffer martyrdom, but the State may not waver."[54] This is rather a strange doctrine to find in the pages of a Christian magazine.

This deification of the state did not find expression in the pages of the *Bibliotheca Sacra* alone. The *New Englander* emphasized the educational rights of the state as something divine. "The state, as the will of the mass impersonated, may, as a divine agent, go by all parents and guardians, over all obstacles . . . till it find the child."[55] The magazine went on to attribute the decline of the common schools of Massachusetts before 1834 to the existence of private schools.

> "Numerous private schools sprang up, and it was found that the public schools were losing their efficiency, and the system itself its vitality." Here is indicated the root of the evil, and one sentence

---

[50] *Loc. cit.*
[51] *Bibliotheca Sacra*, XIII (1856), pp. 725-42.
[52] *Ibid.*, p. 733.
[53] *Loc. cit.*
[54] *Ibid.*, p. 740.
[55] *New Englander*, XVI (1858), p. 854.

declares it . . . The consequences were natural, necessary and full of evil for the community at large.[56]

The writer, however, stopped short of the logical conclusion, that private schools, as sources of public evil, should be abolished.

Before the storm of the Civil War temporarily put a quietus on the question, the *Bibliotheca Sacra* once more discussed "Romanism and the Free Bible."[57] It played variations on the stock themes. "The principal freight of the Mayflower was a free Bible."[58] It was the Bible which made America free and rich. Now the Romanists are attacking the Bible in the common schools. All true Americans should rally to the defense of the Word of God.

A new periodical, the *Congregational Quarterly*, shortly after making its first bow to the public in 1859, joined the Congregationalist chorus in praising the schools of the state. The New England church is particularly interested in popular elementary education, for "free schools are the thought of Puritanism."[59] Congregationalism consequently owes it to itself "to make its commanding influence felt in all the departments of public education."[60]

During the Civil War, Congregationalist periodicals gave little space in their columns to the question of elementary education. The subject reappeared, however, when shortly after Appomattox a national convention of Congregationalists assembled in Boston.

At this conference it was decided to open primary schools under Congregationalist auspices. This decision, however, was not a reversal of Congregationalist policy. The schools were to

---

[56] *Ibid.*, p. 857.
[57] *Bibliotheca Sacra*, XVII (1860), pp. 323-54.
[58] *Ibid.*, p. 323.
[59] *Congregational Quarterly*, III (1861), p. 33.
[60] *Ibid.*, p. 34.

be opened, not in Boston, but in the West. They were to be missionary schools designed to teach true Americanism to those who had come under the influence of "Mormonism" and "Jesuitism." Nor were they to be established where common schools already existed, but only "where the education of the whole population is not provided for by law."[61] The schools were to pass out of existence when the western states had created their systems of public schools.

The council also discussed the question of the Bible in the common schools. It adopted a series of resolutions, praising "our Puritan Fathers" for commanding the daily use of the Holy Scriptures in the schools, regretting any departure from this time-hallowed usage as "destroying the life-giving power of education," and pledging their best efforts to keep the Bible in the schools of the state.[62]

When in 1867 a dispute arose in Connecticut over the question of church schools, the *New Englander* took its stand beside the common schools. It found the arguments of the opposition "decidedly medieval," and the membership of the opposition was not much better. "Generally, though not always, our opponents are of five classes,—grumbling taxpayers, needy gentlefolk, disappointed place-men, ecclesiastical bigots and selfish teachers of private schools."[63] The quarterly found that only in state schools could popular education be secured, and it expressed its distaste for parochial schools, "managed without responsibility to the public, liable to the most bigoted influences and rife in sectarian gall."[64]

---

[61] *Official Record of the National Congregational Council, Boston, 1865*, p. 122 (Boston: Congregational Quarterly, 1865). By 1886 there were 2,560 pupils in 7 academies and 28 free schools under Congregational auspices; *Minutes of National Council, 1886*, p. 171.

[62] *National Congregational Council, 1865*, p. 123.

[63] *New Englander*, XXVI (1867), p. 678.

[64] *Ibid.*, p. 680. .

In the following year the *New Englander* considered the kind of school which the state should conduct.[65] The article, in mentioning resolves introduced into the British Parliament in 1867, showed a tendency to read the present into the past.

> The first resolution is the most significant, for in it, as a careful reader will remark, three principles are laid down, which became part of the fundamental system of New England two hundred years ago. "English instruction must be UNIVERSAL, SECULAR, AND COMPULSORY." This *is* progress![66]

The state, the author found, could conduct four types of schools —"Private, Parish, Pauper or Public."[67] He urged that the first three types be rejected and that his readers support the compulsory education of all children in the fourth.

In 1869 the *Independent* discovered that Catholic parochial schools in New York were receiving state subsidies. Scenting a threat to the public schools, the weekly raised its voice in frequent complaints.[68] Calling the grants "sectarian pilfering," it declared "we should not object to the use of the word *robbery* or *stealing*."[69] It approved state constitutional amendments forbidding such grants, and demanded that the federal constitution be amended in the same fashion.[70] When Senator Blaine and President Grant proposed such an amendment, the *Independent* gladly seconded them.[71]

---

[65] *Ibid.*, XXVII (1868), pp. 99-128.

[66] *Ibid.*, p. 108.

[67] *Ibid.*, p. 111.

[68] *Independent*, May 27, 1869; February 20, May 5, 1870; January 11, February 22, February 29, 1872; January 16, 1873; March 25, April 8, 1875.

[69] *Ibid.*, February 29, 1872.

[70] *Ibid.*, February 22, 1872; January 6, 1876.

[71] *Ibid.*, December 9, December 16, 1875. For Blaine's amendment see Carl Zollman, *American Church Law*, p. 96 (St. Paul: West Publishing Company, 1933). Grant's message will be found in J. D. Richardson, editor, *Messages and Papers of the Presidents*, IX, pp. 4286 ff. (20 vols., New York: Bureau of National Literature, 1897-1917).

Although the *Independent* spoke loudly and often against grants of public money to Catholic schools, it seconded Catholic objections to the use of the King James Version in the common schools even more loudly and more often.[72] Its main contention was that the schools of the secular state should be as secular as the state. "Why should Protestants demand that a chapter of their New Testament should be read every morning in the common schools, any more than in the common post-office, or the common custom-house, or the common law-courts?"[73] The *Independent* condemned as "anti-American and anti-democratic to the very core"[74] a court decision upholding the custom of Bible reading in the Cincinnati public schools. Its stand certainly could not have pleased many of its readers.

While the *Independent* approved Catholic complaints about the reading of the Protestant Bible in public schools, it did not at all approve of Catholic parochial schools. Though it made a grudging admission that the Catholics had a legal right to conduct schools,[75] and though it opened its columns to an explanation of the Catholic position on education by the Catholic bishop, Bernard McQuaid,[76] its own position was clear. A plethora of articles and editorials affirmed the right of the state to control popular elementary education.[77] Many of these articles implied or declared that the control of popular education belonged to

---

[72] *Independent*, November 11, December 30, 1869; January 6, January 13, January 20, January 27, February 24, March 3, July 7, August 18, October 6, 1870; February 23, 1871; January 11, March 28, 1872; April 8, May 20, May 27, 1875; January 6, March 16, 1876.

[73] *Ibid.*, December 30, 1869.

[74] *Ibid.*, October 6, 1870.

[75] *Ibid.*, March 25, 1875.

[76] *Ibid.*, January 13, January 20, 1876.

[77] *Ibid.*, November 4, December 30, 1869; January 6, January 13, January 20, January 27, July 7, 1870; February 2, February 23, 1871; January 11, March 28, 1872; July 23, 1874; March 25, April 8, 1875; January 6, January 20, January 27, February 3, February 10, February 17, March 2, March 16, March 23, April 6, April 13, April 20, April 27, 1876.

the state alone; and many found that the chief enemy of the state systems of public schools was the hierarchy of the Catholic Church.

The Congregationalist quarterlies did not accept the view of the *Independent* that the state schools should be secularized. The *Congregational Quarterly* declared that America recognized Christianity as the religion of the nation and taught that religion, through the medium of the Bible, in the public schools.[78] Nor did the periodical object; the state had the right and the duty to impose her religion on her citizens.[79] In its devotion to religious education in the public schools, it would clothe the secular state in ecclesiastical garments. "The concession to the state of some religious character is the only hope of maintaining the public school system."[80]

The *Bibliotheca Sacra* raised its voice to lament the drift towards secularization.

> Is it safe to fill the land with godless schools, and impart to youth a godless education? Shall we write over every schoolhouse in the land, *No Bible read here, no religious teaching permitted here?*[81]

The *New Englander* published a study of the relations of the church and the state to education.[82] Placing the main responsibility for education on the parents, the quarterly held that both the church and the state had rights in education. It expressed its regret that circumstances would not permit the church to enter the state schools for the purpose of teaching religion.

State education, consequently, was deficient. Therefore the state should leave secondary education to the church, which alone could give a thorough education. Unfortunately, the state

---

[78] *Congregational Quarterly*, XII (1870), p. 528.
[79] *Ibid.*, p. 520.
[80] *Ibid.*, XIII (1871), p. 583. See also *Ibid.*, XV (1873), p. 523.
[81] *Bibliotheca Sacra*, XXVIII (1871), p. 467.
[82] *New Englander*, XXXII (1873), pp. 201-16.

had already begun to overstep its proper bounds; and it was using public funds to destroy church secondary schools.

> The State says, in effect, to Christian parents, that they must not look to it for the complete instruction which their sons and daughters require; but yet they must pay taxes to support the deficient secular system, and make it opulent above all possible rivals.[83]

Since the state cannot teach dogma, it must leave to the church the monopoly of higher education alone. "And then if unbelievers wish for their sons and daughters an education which omits all religious truth, and is 'purely secular' from beginning to end, *let them provide it at their own expense.*"[84] This statement only proves that it all depends on whose ox is gored.

Another issue of the *New Englander*, taking the same position, agreed that the state could tax for the support of public elementary schools, but denied the state the right to levy taxes for the support of public secondary schools.[85]

The centennial year of American independence was the occasion of Congregationalist paeans of praise of that typical American and Protestant institution, the common school.[86] Yet in the next year the *New Englander* felt compelled to defend the church origin of American education against those who insisted that early schools, including Harvard and Yale, were creations of the state rather than of the church.[87] The magazine considered it praiseworthy that the Puritan Church had surrendered control of education to the state.

> It wrought its own free, voluntary element into its beginnings, even when Church and State were one. No other body of Christians ever

---

[83] *Ibid.*, p. 216.
[84] *Loc. cit.*
[85] *Vol. cit.*, pp. 453-67.
[86] *New Englander*, XXXV (1876), p. 650; *Centennial Papers of the General Conference of Connecticut*, p. 177 (Hartford: Case, Lockwood and Brainard Company, 1877).
[87] *New Englander*, XXXVI (1877), pp. 445-86.

did that, as no other ever voluntarily gave up the entire handling of the education of a people.[88]

The following volume of the *New Englander,* however, contained an article which, attacking the thesis of the church origin of American education, also contended that higher education was a function of the state and not of the church.[89]

This latter viewpoint received the official sanction of the Congregational Church. In 1871 was held the first of the regular triennial meetings of the newly created supreme assembly of the Puritan Church, the National Council of Congregational Churches. In 1877 the National Council discussed the question of popular education. It adopted the resolutions expected in Protestant assemblies.[90] It declared that religious training was essential to education. It opposed the division of public funds among sectarian schools. It voted its support to the public schools against the attacks of infidels and Catholics. It called for the retention of the Bible in the state schools. It urged that Congregationalists should use whatever influence they had to secure that end.

More interesting, however, was the acceptance by the National Council of the thesis that secondary education was a function of the state. Indeed, it rather apologetically defended the extant Congregationalist colleges as auxiliaries supplying the deficiencies of state education.

> The matured conviction of the Congregationalist Churches is that, for the promotion of Christian learning, they cannot rely exclusively upon institutions supported and controlled by the State.[91]

The church would therefore continue to conduct its colleges, but it was to be clearly understood that "this policy involves us in

---

[88] *Ibid.,* p. 482.
[89] *Ibid.,* XXXVII (1878), pp. 362-84.
[90] *Minutes of the National Council, 1877,* p. 24.
[91] *Ibid.,* p. 25.

no antagonism to state institutions as such."[92] As to the state colleges, the church heartily desires that they may receive the confidence of all citizens.[93]

A decade later the National Council again turned its attention to the question of Christianity and education. The Reverend George H. Ide addressed the convention on the topic.[94] He argued that, if Christianity is to succeed, it must "lay its hands on the educational forces of the land, and control them measurably."[95] Thus far, the church has been triumphantly successful; all the colleges in the land are Christian. The state has properly assumed control of primary education; but this state control had led to secularization. The church, therefore, must keep control of secondary education to itself. The tendency to relinquish such education to the state must be stopped. The speaker summarized his position succinctly:

> Christian education is an essential part of the work of the Church. To neglect it is to invite defeat. To say that we have nothing else to do but to preach the Gospel, pure and simple, while we leave the question of education to take care of itself, is tantamount to the position that the province of the Church is to Christianize the heart, and the province of the State is to secularize the head.[96]

But the National Council was content to approve the state primary schools and to recommend Christian learning in secondary schools.[97] Obviously the eloquence of the orator had not been suasive enough to lead the council to alter the position it had taken in 1877.

---

[92] *Loc. cit.*

[93] Paul M. Limbert, *Denominational Policies in the Support and Supervision of Higher Education*, p. 60 (New York: Teachers College, Columbia University, 1929), finds this change of opinion on the control of secondary education common among the Protestant churches.

[94] *Minutes of the National Council, 1886*, pp. 238-57.

[95] *Ibid.*, p. 239.

[96] *Ibid.*, p. 257.

[97] *Ibid.*, p. 52.

At the next meeting of the National Council a set address on religion and the public schools was delivered by the Reverend Josiah Strong, a minor prophet of Anglo-Saxon racial superiority.[98] Praising the state schools as pillars of democracy, the speaker criticized the opposition of Catholics and secularists. He called the Catholic Church an anti-American institution whose thesis of church-controlled education "can no more be harmonized with American theory than water can coalesce with oil."[99] Indeed, its parochial schools must necessarily lead to evil results. The answer to the Catholic Church is to improve state schools to such a point that Catholic parents "will refuse to sacrifice the interests of their children at the behests of the priest."[100] To the secularists' objection to the teaching of religion in the public schools, Strong's reiterated answer was that the state must teach religion for its own protection.[101]

With such a spirit present among its members, the National Council voiced its opinion in an intemperate fashion.

Whereas, The authorities of the Roman Catholic Church are making every effort to remove the children of Roman Catholic parents from our public schools, and locate them in parochial schools; are in fact establishing everywhere large parochial schools which threaten to undermine our public school system, and are demanding what they are pleased to call their share of the public funds for the support of parochial schools; therefore

Resolved, That we will firmly and constantly resist every such effort on the part of the Roman Catholic hierarchy to overturn one of our fundamental institutions.

Resolved, That regarding the common public schools as the agency best calculated to unify and make homogeneous the various nationalities that make up our diverse population, we look upon the establishment of parochial schools, where the children of

---

98 *Minutes of the National Council, 1889*, pp. 352-65.
99 *Ibid.*, p. 355.
100 *Ibid.*, p. 356.
101 *Ibid.*, pp. 360, 361, 365.

foreigners are instructed by their teachers and priests, as a just cause of apprehension and a menace to the best interests of our country.

Resolved, That to the last we will withstand the effort to appropriate the public school funds to sectarian purposes, and will insist upon free common school education for the whole American people.[102]

With this resolution of the National Council of Congregational Churches in 1889 may be ended the consideration of the educational thought of the Puritan Church. The Congregational Church never abandoned the traditional position of the Christian Church on the control of popular elementary education. It never took that position. When, after the movement for universal education had attained large proportions, the New England Church first took cognizance of the drive, it accepted, without question, the right of the state to control primary education. Indeed, Congregationalists challenged the right of other churches —the Presbyterian, but chiefly the Catholic—to conduct parochial schools. Not only did the Puritan Church refuse to advance the traditional Christian position on popular education, but it took the further step of denying the right of other Christian churches to advocate and implement that claim.

This Congregationalist stand assumed a new importance when the state began its advance into secondary and higher education. Congregationalist voices were raised to condemn this advance and to assert the sole right of the church to control secondary education. But the Puritan Church soon saw that this position was untenable. Having welcomed the state into the field of education without reservation, it was reduced to justifying its own presence in any part of that field.

---

[102] *Ibid.*, pp. 44-45.

CHAPTER IV

The
Reformed Churches

English Calvinism, which found its major expression in this country under the denominational title of Congregationalism, was but one of the churches originally taking its theology from Geneva. The continental Calvinists have called themselves Reformed, and the Scotch Calvinists have assumed their denominational name from their presbyterian polity.

The major Presbyterian Church experienced a schism in the 1830's. In 1847 the conservative or old-school faction initiated a drive for a system of parochial schools.[1] Although the movement founded about three hundred ephemeral schools, its momentum had been lost by the time of the Civil War, when a sectional schism broke the halves of the church into quarters. Before the old and the new schools in the South reunited in the Presbyterian Church in the United States, and the northern groups formed the Presbyterian Church in the United States of America, the old school had relinquished the Calvinist ideal of education controlled by the church.

---

[1] The story of this movement has been recounted by Lewis J. Sherrill, *Presbyterian Parochial Schools, 1846-1870* (New Haven: Yale University Press, 1932). More details are found in the original manuscript of his doctoral dissertation in the Yale University Library, *Parochial Schools in the Old School Presbyterian Church.*

The Calvinists of continental provenance also had their drives for church elementary schools. Here the most important churches are those known popularly as the Dutch Reformed and the German Reformed. The Dutch Reformed established a national synod in the eighteenth century which met annually. Shortly after the Civil War this synod changed the name of the church from the Reformed Protestant Dutch Church to the Reformed Church in America, by which official title it is still known. The various local synods of the German Reformed Church did not establish a national synod until after the Civil War. This national synod adopted the title of Reformed Church in the United States. By this name it was known until its recent merger in the Evangelical and Reformed Church.[2]

As early as 1809 the Dutch Reformed Church was interested in primary education. In that year the General Synod, appealing to the decrees of the last synod of Dort, declared the education of children of church members to be a matter of primary importance, and asserted the right and duty of the church to inspect all the sources of their instruction.[3] Consequently it devised a plan to set up a complete system of church elementary schools. Local trustees, headed by the pastors, were to establish schools,

---

[2] *The American Church History Series*, VIII (13 vols., New York: Christian Literature Company, 1893-1901), gives brief accounts of both churches. In his treatment of the Dutch Reformed, Edwin T. Corwin ignores popular education. Joseph H. Dobbs notes only that the colonial German Reformed were interested in primary education; *ibid.*, p. 241. Charles E. Corwin, *Manual of the Reformed Church in America*, p. 97 (New York: Board of Publication and Bible-School Work of the Reformed Church in America, 1922), briefly notes interest in parochial schools in 1809 and 1851.

Interestingly enough, the Evangelical Synod, with which the German Reformed merged, also had its movement for parochial schools; see Carl E. Schneider, *The German Church on the American Frontier*, pp. 279-86 (St. Louis: Eden Publishing House, 1939). Another continental Calvinist church, the Christian Reformed Church, still maintains its parochial schools; Rian, *op. cit.,* pp. 208 ff.

[3] *Acts and Proceedings of the General Synod of the Reformed Protestant Dutch Church, 1809*, p. 396.

inspect them, examine and appoint the teachers, and provide for the support of the teachers and the schools.[4]

While the enactments of the General Synod were emphasized by reaffirming *in toto* the legislation of 1809 at the convention of 1814, the laws apparently were never applied.[5] For a generation thereafter, the General Synod did not mention the subject of elementary education. Indeed, it was not until 1843 that general education was once more introduced at the meetings of the General Synod. In that year the Dutch Reformed urged their missionaries on the western frontier to exert their influence towards the establishment and support of Christian schools.[6]

Three years later the General Synod received complaints that books in the common-school libraries were "subversive of pure and sound Christianity."[7] The Committee on Education, however, while it declared that the church should take note of the matter, sounded a warning that "the Synod should be careful not to interfere with the business of the state."[8] Thus in its first statement touching on common schools the Synod of the Dutch Reformed Church conceded to the state the right to control popular elementary education.

This position received support in 1849 in the first volume of the most influential of the Reformed quarterlies, the *Mercersburg Review*. This organ of the German Reformed found the state to be "constitutionally a divine power, having all the functions and characteristics of a religious institution."[9] Among the functions pertaining to this ecclesiastical state was "the edu-

---

4 *Ibid.*, p. 398.
5 *Ibid.*, *1814*, pp. 79-83.
6 *Ibid.*, *1843*, p. 232.
7 *Ibid.*, *1846*, p. 71.
8 *Ibid.*, p. 73.
9 *Mercersburg Review*, I (1849), p. 573. This quarterly, now known as the *Reformed Church Review*, was entitled the *Mercersburg Review* for practically the whole period with which this study is concerned. Consequently it will be cited under its original title.

cational."[10] The article argued that the ideal relationship of church and state was one of union, almost of identity. "They are one, but yet distinct."[11] It declared that "in the Church, and in the Church alone, can the State reach her ideal perfection."[12] If there was any question of which church should be united to the state in America, the *Mercersburg Review* shortly thereafter dissipated the doubt. An article endeavored to determine our national religion, and found that "our Government is committed in favor of that system of religion which characterizes Protestant Evangelical Christianity."[13]

In the meantime the most influential of the Dutch Reformed weeklies, the *Christian Intelligencer*, was having qualms about leaving the education of Reformed children in the hands of this Protestant Evangelical state. It studied the old-school Presbyterian movement for parochial schools, and asked why the Dutch Reformed should not follow their example.[14] The *Intelligencer* did not question the right of the state to offer primary education. Indeed, it published several articles praising the common schools of New York City,[15] but it thought elementary schools conducted by the church a more excellent way.[16]

The efforts of the *Intelligencer* for parochial schools were not without results. The General Synod appointed a committee on education, whose report declared for church schools on the authority of the Synod of Dort, and the higher authority of the commission given to the church to teach all nations.[17] While the committee had no doubt of the propriety and practicability of

---

[10] *Loc. cit.*
[11] *Ibid.,* p. 577.
[12] *Loc. cit.*
[13] *Ibid.,* III (1851), p. 327.
[14] *Christian Intelligencer,* January 30, 1851.
[15] *Ibid.,* November 20, 1851; April 8, April 15, April 29, 1852.
[16] *Ibid.,* January 30, September 18, December 18, 1851; August 12, 1852.
[17] *Acts and Proceedings, 1852,* p. 268.

parochial schools, it felt that the local Classes should express
their views in the next General Synod on the utility of church-
controlled schools.[18]

In the same year the Synod of the German Reformed in
Baltimore listened to a sermon on parochial schools delivered by
the Reverend H. Harbaugh which excited such interest that the
Mercersburg Review published a revised version.[19] The orator,
discovering four systems of popular education, rejected out of
hand the "Pagan System" of the ancients and the "Infidel System" of Rousseau. The third system, under which the American
common schools fitted, the preacher treated at some length, "for
it stands more directly and more formidably than all the others
in the way of Parochial or Christian schools."[20] He found the
Prussian public schools, with their religious education, more
laudable than the American common schools, but he preferred
above all a system of church schools.

For some time the *Christian Intelligencer* continued its campaign for parochial schools,[21] but early in 1853 the magazine
began to reverse its policy. It had discovered the Catholic threat
to the state schools. Soon it was publishing defenses of the common schools and questioning the value of parochial schools.[22]

In the meanwhile the annual General Synod of the Dutch
Church had convened. The Committee on Education reported
that two Particular Synods, those of Albany and New York, had
voiced unanimous disbelief in the practicability of parochial
schools.[23] The committee expressed its belief that this, in itself,

---

[18] *Ibid.*, p. 269. The Classes and the Particular Synod were intermediate assemblies
between the local congregation and the General Synod.
[19] *Mercersburg Review*, V (1853), pp. 23-50.
[20] *Ibid.*, p. 32.
[21] *Christian Intelligencer*, November 11, 1852; January 27, February 3, March 3,
1853.
[22] *Ibid.*, March 17, April 7, April 21, October 21, November 3, 1853.
[23] *Acts and Proceedings, 1853*, p. 359.

was sufficient evidence that the General Synod should not press the matter further. Consequently, while noting appreciatively the gift of $7,000 by a layman of the church to aid in the establishment of parochial schools, it could not recommend its acceptance. The report summed up:

> The system of common schools at present prevailing in our country, and in which the Bible is read and our common Christianity acknowledged, is productive of incalculable good; and your Committee are persuaded that the establishment of parochial schools throughout the Churches would essentially, if not fatally, interfere with it.
>
> Your Committee are firmly persuaded that, while the State does not interfere with the appropriate duties of the Church, the Church, on the contrary ought not to adopt any measure which will interfere with the interests to which the State is giving commendable attention, and which properly belong to her in her civil capacity.[24]

The *Mercersburg Review* also agreed that the state should provide for universal primary education,[25] but it insisted that this education be religious.[26]

In the year after the synod of 1853 the Dutch Reformed had time for sober second thoughts, which caused the reversal, in the General Synod of 1854, of the stand previously taken on parochial schools. Indeed, the old ideal of a school beside every church stirred beneath its tombstone. The report of the Committee on Education foresaw the day when parochial schools "may, and will, become an important feature in our educational system."[27]

The committee stated the two main objections to a system of parochial schools, which were now happily dissipated: that it

---

[24] *Ibid.,* p. 360.
[25] *Mercersburg Review,* VI (1854), p. 284.
[26] *Ibid.,* p. 291.
[27] *Acts and Proceedings, 1854,* p. 454.

"might interfere with our public school system, and that it might furnish a plea to the Romanists for claiming a share of the public money."[28] On the contrary, the committee asserted, the church schools would exert a wholesome influence, by salutary competition, on the state schools. Furthermore, since the Dutch Church would pay for its own schools and reject state money even if it were offered, it would deprive the Catholics of all pretexts for claims on the public treasury.

As a result of this action of the General Synod of 1854 a number of churches were able to report the establishment of parochial schools to the next General Synod.[29] By 1856 seven parochial schools were receiving subsidies from the Board of Education of the Dutch Church.[30]

In subsequent years the General Synod repeated its blessing on the parochial schools, usually with a lament on the lack of interest shown in the schools by its congregations.[31] Soon it discovered that only churches composed of recent immigrants from Europe were maintaining church schools.[32] Finally, in 1866, the General Synod repudiated the ideal of a system of Dutch Reformed parochial schools.[33] It declared that, although they were in some cases desirable, parochial schools should be the exception rather than the rule; nor should they be allowed to come into competition with the public schools. After this declaration the Dutch Reformed General Synod largely ignored the question of church-controlled primary education.[34]

---

28 *Ibid.*, p. 455.
29 *Ibid., 1855*, p. 580.
30 *Ibid., 1856*, p. 98. Each Protestant church commonly had, as did the Dutch Reformed, a permanent board of education to assist candidates for the ministry. The Committee on Education was a temporary organ of the General Synod.
31 *Ibid., 1857*, p. 196; *1859*, p. 436; *1861*, p. 73; *1862*, p. 184; *1863*, p. 318; *1864*, p. 466.
32 *Ibid., 1862*, p. 184; *1863*, p. 318.
33 *Ibid., 1866*, p. 88.
34 Passing mention was given *ibid., 1867*, p. 244; *1869*, p. 642.

The number of schools subsidized by the Board of Education reached twenty in 1859;[35] thereafter the number steadily declined. Though the board itself continued to campaign for parochial schools until 1873, it then wrote finis to the effort for Reformed parochial schools.[36] Nor did the *Christian Intelligencer* regret the disappearance of the Dutch Reformed schools. Indeed, its comments on elementary education were largely confined to attacks on the position of the Catholic Church.[37]

While the Dutch Reformed were rejecting church control of primary education, the new General Synod of the German Reformed was announcing a growing interest in parochial schools.[38] The *Mercersburg Review* did its bit to increase that interest. Its editor, the Reverend T. G. Apple, although praising the state schools, regretted their secularization.[39]

> What we do complain of, and what we do regard as a startling fact, is that during all this time the Church has done so little directly in the interest of general education. She has coolly stood aloof and allowed the State to take her little ones from her bosom and train them up in a step-motherly way.[40]

Apple's demand for parochial schools was reiterated in another article in the *Review*.[41] A third article explained the educational policy of the periodical.[42] While opposing such union of church and state as obtained in several European countries, the maga-

---

[35] *Ibid., 1859*, p. 436. For a number of years the Board of Education continued to list the schools in its annual reports. Five were still in being in 1879; *Forty-seventh Annual Report*, p. 4. The Board, in its *Semicentennial Report* surveying all work done up to 1882, completely ignored the parochial school.

[36] *Forty-first Annual Report*, p. 11.

[37] *Christian Intelligencer*, December 23, 1873; April 2, 1874; September 2, 1875; January 6, 1876.

[38] *Acts and Proceedings of the General Synod of the German Reformed Church, 1866*, p. 87.

[39] *Mercersburg Review*, XVI (1869), pp. 5-24.

[40] *Ibid.*, p. 9.

[41] *Ibid.*, XVII (1870), pp. 150-55.

[42] *Ibid.*, XIX (1872), pp. 153-57.

zine advocated cooperation between church and state in the
field of elementary education, and demanded that the church
be granted a monopoly of secondary instruction.

That the demand of the *Mercersburg Review* for parochial
schools had not fallen on deaf ears is shown by the fact that the
German General Synod of 1875 ordered its Committee on the
Revision of the Constitution to provide articles "that refer to
the establishment and maintenance of Parochial Schools."[43] Although the report of the committee in 1878 did not touch upon
the subject,[44] the constitution submitted in 1881 provided that
"every congregation shall provide properly for the support
of . . . the parochial school, wherever such a school is practicable."[45] Since that particular section was omitted from later
proposed constitutions, no further reference to parochial schools
is found.[46]

The *Mercersburg Review* began to alter its opinion on the
control of popular elementary education. In 1878 the magazine
published an article on the state elementary schools which was
an uninterrupted paean of praise.[47] Only on the last page was
the question of religion raised. Then the writer declared that,
since the American government was Christian, its education
should also be Christian; and its education would be Christian
if the Bible were retained in the state schools.

The following number of the magazine discussed the relationship of religion to the state.[48] The author approved the principle of the separation of church and state, but he held the
decidedly Erastian viewpoint that the church, separated from
the state, should be subservient to it; the church "can never

---

43 *Reformed Church in the United States, Acts, 1875,* p. 54.
44 *Ibid.,* 1878, pp. 64-68.
45 *Ibid.,* 1881, p. 127.
46 *Ibid.,* 1887, pp. 107-41; *1893,* pp. 165-92.
47 *Mercersburg Review,* XXV (1878), pp. 508-23.
48 *Ibid.,* pp. 545-60.

rightly array itself against the State."[49] On the question of education the writer expressed the opinion that state neutrality to religion was not only undesirable but impossible. "In reality, we may be said to be, as a nation, not only Christian but even Protestant."[50] Consequently, while the Bible should not be forced into the public schools nor formal religious education be imposed, the state is justified in banning from the common schools books inimical to the Christian Church and teachers opposed to religion.[51]

In 1880 the *Mercersburg Review* investigated the peril to free institutions from "Romanism."[52] In general, the article found little to fear from a moribund institution; "the Vatican Council was but a dying spasm, the summoning of its waning strength for a final curse and a final stab."[53] It hailed, as one of the main causes of the decline of the Catholic Church, the American system of popular education, which "is sweeping each generation farther away from Rome."[54]

The new policy of the *Mercersburg Review* on the control of primary education was emphasized by an article published in 1882. The author expressed his pleasure in the fact that state elementary schools were now universal throughout the United States. He announced that "private schools and academies have had their day."[55] He believed, however, that the state should allow the church an unquestioned monopoly of collegiate education. Fervently he wished that "God save this commonwealth from anything like a State university!"[56]

---

[49] *Ibid.*, p. 552.
[50] *Ibid.*, p. 553.
[51] *Ibid.*, p. 557.
[52] *Ibid.*, XXVII (1880), pp. 444-60. The article was written by an editor of the *Christian Intelligencer*.
[53] *Mercersburg Review, vol. cit.*, p. 457.
[54] *Loc. cit.*
[55] *Ibid.*, XXIX (1882), p. 263.
[56] *Ibid.*, p. 277.

In the following year the Reformed quarterly took exception to a proposal in the *Atlantic Monthly* that the state schools teach a morality based on a rational, non-Christian philosophy. The *Mercersburg Review* argued that, as a Christian nation, this state must teach a Christian morality in its schools.[57] This teaching of Christianity, "already in vogue to so large an extent in the Common Schools of our land,"[58] should not, the magazine held, "be confounded with the teaching of theological doctrines and abstract dogmas."[59] Instruction in the doctrines of a particular church should be left to the ministers and the Sunday schools of the church in question.

The reversal of the educational policy of the *Mercersburg Review* is further underlined by an article written in 1884 by its editor, the Reverend T. G. Apple. In 1869 he had published an article demanding that the German Reformed Church establish parochial schools.[60] Fifteen years later Apple still maintained that the only complete solution to the problem of the control of popular education would be "in a theocracy, in which Church and State are one."[61] But since that solution was presently impossible, he was content to accept the best practicable solution in the existing state of affairs—and that was to leave the control of popular primary education to the state. He spurned the theory that the church alone should control elementary education as a relic of the Middle Ages and as a theory held only by the Catholic Church. Yet he wanted the church to continue its control of higher education; for he believed that, as long as the colleges were Christian, so too would be the elementary education controlled exclusively by the state.[62]

---

[57] *Ibid.*, XXX (1883), pp. 472-74.
[58] *Ibid.*, p. 483.
[59] *Ibid.*, p. 480.
[60] *Vide supra*, note 39.
[61] *Mercersburg Review*, XXXI (1884), p. 289.
[62] *Ibid.*, p. 291.

Thus did the last champion of parochial schools within the Calvinistic denominations relinquish the Christian claim to control popular elementary education.

It was not until mid-century that the Calvinistic churches opened their drives for parochial schools, drives that were largely an adverse reaction to the common schools of the state. When the churches moved, the state was already in possession. The efforts of the churches came too late. Their members, in the absence of church schools, had accepted the schools of the state. Their acceptance became devotion, as the Reformed rallied to the defense of the state schools against the supposed attacks of infidels and Catholics. While they did not formally reject it, the Reformed churches silently abandoned the claim of the Christian Church to control popular elementary education.

CHAPTER V

The
Quakers

The concern for education of the Society of Friends has a long and honorable history. The founder of the Quaker denomination, George Fox, himself established schools, and English Quakers as early as 1690 were urging their coreligionists to follow his example.[1]

On the other hand, some of the most famous Quakers in the British colonies advocated the control of popular education, not by the church, but by the state. William Penn himself wrote that opinion into the fundamental laws of his colony of Pennsylvania. While the Charter of Privileges which he granted to the colonists in 1701 made no mention of education, the three earlier Frames of Government, which he promulgated for Pennsylvania in 1682, 1683, and 1696, all had clauses which reserved to the state the control of education.[2] Two other famous colonial Friends, John Woolman and Anthony Bezenet, also believed that the control of education should be vested in the state.[3]

---

[1] Howard H. Brinton, *Quaker Education*, p. 33 (Wallingford: Pendle Hill Press, 1940); Thomas S. Woody, *Early Quaker Education in Pennsylvania*, pp. 7 ff. (New York: Teachers College, Columbia University, 1920).

[2] Francis N. Thorpe, editor, *Federal and State Constitutions*, V, cols. 3056, 3066, 3074. 7 vols., Washington: Government Printing Office, 1909.

[3] Woody, *op. cit.*, pp. 30 ff.

In spite of the opinions of their most prominent leaders, the Society of Friends, when once it was clear that the colonial governments were not going to supply the means of education, established elementary schools under the control of their church.[4]

When American independence had been achieved, the Quakers continued their support of elementary education. Indeed, the period about the year 1800 saw the apogee of the Friends' interest in the primary teaching of their children.[5] Under the supervision of the Philadelphia Yearly Meeting there were, near the beginning of the nineteenth century, between sixty and seventy parochial schools in Pennsylvania and another thirty or thirty-five in New Jersey.[6]

Their experience with—to use their own phrase—"the guarded religious education" of their children in elementary schools under the supervision of their own religious organization apparently convinced the Friends that, in this matter of education, the opinion of Penn, Bezenet, and Woolman was not the policy to follow.

When, then, the movement for universal elementary education developed in the second quarter of the nineteenth century, the minutes of the various yearly meetings manifested Quaker determination to keep the control of the education of their children out of the hands of the state, and firmly in the grip of their denomination.[7]

---

[4] Elbert Russell, *History of Quakerism*, p. 207 (New York: The Macmillan Company, 1942) ; Woody, *op. cit.*, p. 270; Brinton, *op. cit.*, p. 39.

[5] Thomas S. Woody, editor, *Quaker Education in the Colony and State of New Jersey*, p. 376 (Philadelphia: University of Pennsylvania, 1923) ; Russell, *op. cit.*, p. 400; Brinton, *op. cit.*, p. 41.

[6] Brinton, *op. cit.*, p. 39; Woody, *Early Quaker Education in Pennsylvania*, p. 271.
  It is well known that the Society of Friends had no national organization. The local Preparatory, Monthly, and Quarterly Meetings were grouped together under various regional Yearly Meetings.

[7] Woody, *Quaker Education in the Colony and State of New Jersey*, p. 30; Zora Klain, editor, *Educational Activities of New England Quakers*, pp. 20-23 (Philadelphia: Westbrook Publishing Company, 1928).

This resolution was not an easy one to implement. The Hicksite schism, which began in the Philadelphia yearly meeting towards the end of the 1820's, opened elementary schools in competition with extant Friends' schools.[8] The peculiar organization of the Society of Friends, however, made this duplication of facilities but a local problem. The regional grouping of the Quakers made the Hicksite schism regional; while it split the Philadelphia yearly meeting into opposed orthodox and Hicksite sects, it did not touch the Society of Friends in New England.

Even apart from this schism, the determination of the Friends to control elementary education faced difficulties. In 1834 preparatory and monthly meetings reported to the orthodox yearly meeting of Philadelphia that many Quaker congregations could not conduct elementary schools, for a number of reasons which were to recur continually in Quaker documents.[9] In many localities the Friends were too few and too widely scattered to permit of the establishment of a Quaker school. Where schools could be set up, competent Quaker teachers were not to be had. Where there were Friends' schools, many Quaker parents preferred to send their children to the state schools rather than undertake the extra expense of a guarded religious education. In the same year the Hicksite yearly meeting of Philadelphia issued a report on education noting precisely the same difficulties.[10]

Nevertheless both the orthodox and the Hicksite groups in the Middle States continued to urge the maintenance of what Friends' schools existed and the establishment of new ones. In this they were joined by the yearly meeting of the New England Society of Friends, which urged its membership to look to the creation of Friends' schools wherever such institutions were

---

[8] Brinton, *op. cit.*, p. 41; Woody, *Quaker Education in the Colony and State of New Jersey*, p. 377.

[9] Woody, *Quaker Education in the Colony and State of New Jersey*, p. 27.

[10] *Ibid.*, p. 32; William C. Dunlap, *Quaker Education in Baltimore and Virginia Yearly Meetings*, p. 12 (Philadelphia: The Author, 1936).

practicable.[11] To spur on this work the New England yearly meeting, as did the other annual assemblies, advanced the widely held belief that the schools of the state were dangerous to the faith of Quaker children.[12]

The situation of the Friends' schools became even more difficult when taxation was employed by the state to finance the establishment and maintenance of systems of common schools. Quaker meetings had to report that many Friends were unwilling to assume the burden of a double educational levy, the taxes of the state and the fees of the church school.[13]

Still the concern for the guarded religious education of their children was sustained, not only in the older strongholds of the Friends, but also in territories where the Society of Friends was far less numerous and influential. In North Carolina, for example, the Quakers during the forties supported fourteen elementary schools.[14] On the new lands of the trans-Allegheny frontier the Indiana yearly meeting had, by 1850, ninety-six primary schools under its supervision and control.[15]

Nor did the Civil War witness a decline of Quaker activity in denominational elementary education. Indeed, the period of Reconstruction saw an increased interest in Quaker primary schools. In North Carolina the Friends' elementary schools, which had declined in number to four by 1861, mounted to forty-three in 1870, and still numbered thirty-nine as late as 1886.[16] The New England yearly meeting could report in 1871 that 34 per cent of all Quaker children within its boundaries

---

[11] Klain, *Educational Activities of New England Quakers*, pp. 20, 23.
[12] *Loc. cit.*; Woody, *Quaker Education in the Colony and State of New Jersey,* pp. 30, 362.
[13] Woody, *Quaker Education in the Colony and State of New Jersey*, p. 363.
[14] Zora Klain, *Quaker Contributions to Education in North Carolina*, pp. 68, 280. Philadelphia: The Author, 1924.
[15] Brinton, *op. cit.,* p. 41.
[16] Klain, *Quaker Contributions to Education in North Carolina*, p. 32.

between the ages of five and twenty-one were in schools controlled by the Friends.[17] The Hicksite yearly meeting of Philadelphia, however, noticed in 1873 a decline in the number of
elementary schools under their supervision. That they had not
yet surrendered the traditional claim of the Christian Church to
control education is indicated by the fact that they urged the
local congregations to exert their best efforts to maintain the
Friends' schools.[18]

The period of Reconstruction also witnessed new efforts for
church elementary schools by the yearly meeting of Baltimore.
A survey disclosed that there were in 1875 but three primary
schools under the control of the meeting, but that every local
congregation expressed the desire to have a parochial school. The
Baltimore meeting consequently set up a committee on education to deal with the problem.[19] The committee set, as the ideal
to be striven for by the Society of Friends, the traditional Christian standard, to have "in our Society a system of schools beginning at the lowest Primary Schools and going up the various
grades to the highest."[20] While this lofty aim was never even
approximated by the Baltimore yearly meeting, nevertheless
something was accomplished. By 1885 the three Friends' elementary schools had become fifteen, and the Committee on Education could proudly report that "there has not been a time
before this when more interest was felt in the matter of education by our members. . . . This interest is extending and in-
tensifying throughout our borders."[21]

If the year 1885 marked a high point in Quaker interest in
church-controlled popular education, the collapse came very
shortly thereafter. Reports from various sections of the country

---

[17] Klain, *Educational Activities of New England Quakers*, p. 32.
[18] Woody, *Quaker Education in the Colony and State of New Jersey*, p. 34.
[19] Dunlap, *op. cit.*, p. 14.
[20] *Ibid.*, p. 15.
[21] *Ibid.*, p. 25.

showed that the number of Friends' schools had diminished with a notable rapidity. Of the ninety-six elementary schools controlled by the Indiana yearly meeting at mid-century, not one was left by 1890.[22] The Quaker schools in North Carolina, which numbered thirty-nine in 1885, dropped to twelve by 1895, and to four by 1905.[23] The yearly meeting of the Society of Friends in New England had in 1902 but fifty-two pupils in Quaker primary schools.[24] Even in the yearly meeting of Baltimore, where enthusiasm ran so high in 1885 over the fifteen Friends' schools, only two schools remained in 1906.[25] Only a handful of the Quaker schools survived the sudden collapse.

It is clear that, by the dawn of the twentieth century, the efforts of the Society of Friends to control the elementary education of Quaker children were, for all practical purposes, defeated.

In this final collapse of Quaker attempts to fulfill the traditional educational aim of the Christian Church, the factors which hindered the progress of earlier Quaker efforts were still operative, and probably more effective. The Society of Friends has never had a numerous church membership. Nor, after the first flush of fervor in Fox's day, had they made strenuous attempts to increase their membership by proselytizing among their neighbors. Consequently, in the multiplying population of nineteenth-century America, Quakerism suffered a very marked relative decline in numerical strength. If in the 1830's Quaker congregations were unable to sustain denominational primary schools because their members were too few and too widely scattered, by the 1890's the situation was even more impossible. Nor did the Friends ever attempt to solve, by the establishment

---

[22] Brinton, *op. cit.*, p. 42.
[23] Klain, *Quaker Contributions to Education in North Carolina*, p. 280.
[24] Klain, *Educational Activities of New England Quakers*, p. 25.
[25] Dunlap, *op. cit.*, p. 25.

of normal schools or other means, the problem of the shortage
of trained Quaker teachers for their elementary schools.

Possibly more important than fewness of numbers and lack
of teachers was the reluctance of many Quakers to finance the
guarded religious education of Friends' children. From all sections which once boasted Quaker elementary schools came reports of the unwillingness of members of the Society to bear a
double school tax.[26]

Another element in the collapse of the Friends' attempt to
control education was a declining interest in Quaker doctrine.
As a consequence of the liberalizing of dogma the Baltimore
yearly meeting could declare that "there does not seem to be
need for separate schools for Friends at present."[27] The New
England yearly meeting could even speak of Quaker schools as
"sectarian nurseries," and assert that "the advantages of a
Friends' school are small in the direction of Denominational
Education."[28] The same meeting approvingly declared that "the
present tendency of all denominations is to take down their denominational bounds and hedges, and to recognize and cherish,
everywhere, the brethren of the Church Universal, rather than
the more selfish interests of their sect."[29] When Quaker belief
had reached that point, the very *raison d'etre* of Friends' schools
had vanished.

---

[26] Russell, *op. cit.*, p. 450; Woody, *Quaker Education in the Colony and State of
New Jersey*, pp. 363, 377; Dunlap, *op. cit.*, p. 25; Brinton, *op. cit.*, p. 41.
[27] Dunlap, *op. cit.*, p. 25.
[28] Klain, *Educational Activities of New England Quakers*, p. 33.
[29] *Loc. cit.*

CHAPTER VI

The
Methodists

The founders of Methodism believed that the elementary education of Methodist children under the control of the Church was an important part of their work. As the latest historian of Methodism writes, "Wesley resolutely took the stand that education should be made available for all . . . and he resolutely led the way."[1] During his sojourn in the colony of Georgia, John Wesley established a school.[2] Later George Whitefield, in the same colony, also endeavored to set up schools.[3] In England, Wesley continued his interest in primary education; he founded a school in London[4] and supported a school, well known in Methodist annals, at Kingswood.[5]

The patriarch of Methodism passed his interest in church-controlled elementary education on to his English followers. In the twenty years before our Civil War, while the American Methodists were concentrating their educational endeavors on

---

[1] Wade C. Barclay, *Early American Methodism*, I, p. xxxi. 2 vols., New York: Board of Missions and Church Extension of the Methodist Church, 1949.

[2] Alfred H. Body, *John Wesley and Education*, p. 69. London: Epworth Press, 1936.

[3] *Ibid.*, p. 72.

[4] Barclay, *op. cit.*, I, p. xxxi.

[5] Maximin Piette, *John Wesley*, p. 391. New York: Sheed and Ward, 1937.

the field of secondary education, the English Methodists were busily providing, throughout the length and breadth of England, some seven hundred elementary schools controlled by their church organizations.[6]

When, after the American Revolution, the Methodists in the new United States were beginning their work of organization and expansion, Methodist leaders were interested in the problems of elementary education. The greatest figure in early American Methodism, Bishop Francis Asbury, was especially concerned. In 1791 he wrote an encyclical letter to the Methodist Church, in which he urged his coreligionists "as your duty and privilege, to give the key of knowledge in a general way to your children and those of the poor in the vicinity of your small towns and villages."[7] He proposed that every Methodist congregation should, if possible, establish a parochial school, in order that their children might learn their letters in a religious atmosphere. He expressed the conviction that "we have small hopes of coming properly at the lambs of the flock, till you have schools of your own founding, and under your own direction, that neither ourselves nor the teachers may be under any restraints from refractory men."[8]

This early Methodist interest in education led to the establishment of a number of short-lived schools.[9] The most important of these was Cokesbury College, established near Baltimore in 1787 and named after Asbury and his fellow bishop Coke. The

---

[6] Body, *op. cit.*, p. 9. Cubberley, *History of Education*, p. 632, however, lists only 363 Wesleyan schools.

[7] *Minutes Taken at the Several Conferences of the Methodist Episcopal Church in America for 1792*, p. 17. Philadelphia: Parry Hall, 1792.

[8] *Loc. cit.*

[9] Sylvanus M. Duvall, *The Methodist Episcopal Church and Education up to 1869*, p. 36 (New York: Teachers College, Columbia University, 1929); A. W. Cummings, *Early Schools of Methodism*, pp. 18 ff. (New York: Phillips and Hunt, 1886); Albea Godbold, *The Church College of the Old South*, p. 31 (Durham: Duke University Press, 1944).

curriculum of the college, which included reading, writing, and arithmetic, indicates that it had an elementary department.[10]

That the attempt to found secondary rather than primary schools was a departure from the aims of the leaders of Methodism is attested by both Wesley and Asbury. Asbury confided to his journal that "the Lord called not Mr. Whitefield nor the Methodists to build colleges. I wished only for schools—Dr. Coke wanted a college."[11] Wesley sent a letter to his "dear Franky," admonishing him:

> I study to be little, you study to be great. I creep; you strut along. I found a school; you a college: nay, and call it after your own names. O beware, do not seek to be something![12]

Apparently Wesley's wrath called down fires from heaven, for two conflagrations soon brought a permanent end to Cokesbury College and temporarily extinguished Methodist interest in church schools.[13]

Before the college was abandoned the first of the quadrennial Methodist general conferences, which was held in 1796, reflected the early Methodist interest in general education. This supreme governing body of the Methodist Episcopal Church enacted a series of regulations entitled "The Plan of Education Recommended to All Our Seminaries of Learning." To modern educators some details would be entrancing. Teachers were instructed to "prohibit *play* in the strongest terms; and in this we have the two greatest writers on the subject that perhaps any age has produced—Mr. Locke and M. Rousseau—of our senti-

---

10 Duvall, *op. cit.*, p. 34.
11 Francis Asbury, *Journal,* III, p. 287. 3 vols., New York: Eaton and Mains, n.d.
12 Body, *op. cit.*, p. 28.
13 Abel Stevens, *History of the Methodist Episcopal Church in the United States,* II, p. 259 (4 vols., New York: Carlton and Porter, 1866-1867) ; Nathan Bangs, *History of the Methodist Episcopal Church,* II, p. 413 (4 vols., New York: Mason and Lane, 1840) ; P. Douglass Gorrie, *Episcopal Methodism,* p. 67 (Auburn: Miller, Orton and Mulligan, 1854).

ments."[14] To dignify manual labor, which was highly recommended, an appeal was made to the example of "the greatest statesman that perhaps ever shone in the annals of history, *Peter*, the Russian emperor, who was deservedly styled *the Great*, [who] disdained not to stoop to the employment of a *ship-carpenter*."[15] Bathing was to be permitted as a recreation, but "only one shall bathe at a time; and no one shall remain in the water above a minute." Troublemakers were provided for; in each school "a convenient room shall be set apart as a place of confinement."[16]

After the enactment of this plan of education the General Conference maintained an absolute silence on the subject of education until the assembly was called to order in 1820. In that year education was reintroduced, and thereafter it was usually part of the agenda of the quadrennial Conference.[17]

Although education in general was commended, and secondary and theological educational institutions were discussed in some detail, the General Conference rarely touched upon the question of popular elementary education. Indeed, the matter was not even mentioned before the Conference of 1832; and then it received but a passing reference. The journal of the General Conference reported that a communication "on the subject of infant and early education" had been presented to the assembly and referred to the Committee on Education.[18] There, apparently, it died; no further mention of the matter is made.

The question of popular primary education did, however, receive some attention in the columns of the *Christian Advocate*. This periodical, published in New York City, had the largest

---

[14] *Journals of the General Conferences of the Methodist Episcopal Church, 1796-1836*, p. 18.
[15] *Loc. cit.*
[16] *Ibid.*, pp. 19-20.
[17] *Ibid.*, pp. 186, 208, 296, 403, *et passim*.
[18] *Ibid.*, p. 403.

circulation and the greatest influence of the Methodist weekly journals of opinion. Its standing as an official organ of the Methodist Episcopal Church is attested by the fact that the selection of its editor, alone of the Methodist weeklies, was reserved to the General Conference.

In the early years of the thirties the *Christian Advocate* published a number of articles urging its readers to exert Methodist influence on the common schools.[19] Indeed, in one issue the magazine called for the creation of a complete system of education under the sole control of the Methodist Church.[20] This demand apparently fell on deaf ears; nothing more was heard about the matter. This call for Methodist parochial schools was almost unique in the history of Methodism.

Other Methodist organizations, however, added their voices to that of the *Christian Advocate* in demands that church members increase the influence of the Methodist Church on popular education. The Methodist Annual Conference of Philadelphia urged, in 1835, that Wesley's denomination set about the preparation of thousands of young Methodists for teaching positions in the common schools and academies.[21] The Committee on Education of the General Conference of 1836, advising ministers to visit and influence the state schools, declared that the question of primary schools ought to be made a subject of special interest to the Methodist Church.[22]

Later in the thirties the *Christian Advocate* published a series of articles on the question of popular elementary education.[23] The weekly gave its blessing to the schools of the state. It declared that, since the common schools could reach all American

---

19 *Christian Advocate*, October 8, 1830; February 11, 1831; April 6, 1833; February 21, 1834; January 3, 1835.
20 *Ibid.*, April 6, 1833.
21 *Ibid.*, May 1, 1835.
22 *Ibid.*, June 24, 1836.
23 *Ibid.*, March 9, March 23, March 30, April 13, 1838.

children, on these schools rested the duty of the religious education of those children.[24]

The *Christian Advocate* did not consider, even if only to reject, Methodist parochial schools as a means of religious training. Methodism, it would appear, was already committed to the
proposition that the control of popular elementary education
belonged solely to the state.

There were, however, one or two indications that the traditional claim of the Christian Church to control primary education had not completely vanished from the memory of the
Wesleyan Church. The Reverend (later Bishop) Edmund S.
Janes celebrated the centenary of Methodism by an address on
education, in which he stressed its necessity to the Methodist
Episcopal Church.

> Neither does the fact that the powerful influence of education has
> been seized upon by the wicked and made to subserve their base
> purposes, lessen its value. On the contrary, the fact that this tre-
> mendous power may be laid hold of by bad men, and employed in
> the service of sin, makes it, to the Church, a subject of momentous
> concern. The question is simply this: Who shall possess and exert
> this power? Shall it be yielded to the irreligious, to infidels, to
> Roman Catholics? Shall they employ it in the service of Antichrist,
> and in the overthrow of Christianity? No, in the name of God, we
> say, No![25]

The future bishop went on to urge that the Methodist Church
enter wholeheartedly into the work of education and erect a
complete system of church schools, both secondary and primary.
He declared the church recreant to her high responsibilities and
destinies if it did not provide these schools. "Fearful will be her
reckoning, if, with her means and opportunities, she fails to
furnish her children with abundant advantages for obtaining

---

[24] *Ibid.*, April 13, 1838.
[25] *Methodist Quarterly Review*, XXII (1840), p. 404.

common and liberal education, under moral and religious influences."[26] This unusual appeal had no more effect than the similar appeal by the *Christian Advocate*.

The Catholic threat, mentioned in Janes' address, soon became a common, if not the central, topic in Methodist discussions of elementary education. The Baltimore Annual Conference of 1840 passed resolutions demanding the retention of the Bible in the state schools, and condemning those Protestants who sent their children to Catholic schools "from which the Holy Scriptures are excluded."[27]

During the decade of the forties the *Christian Advocate* was strenuous in rebutting Catholic complaints about conditions in the common schools of New York City. It castigated objections to the King James Version as "the artful policy employed by the enemies of our common Christianity to exclude the sacred volume from a place among the books of instruction in our schools."[28] While the alleged Catholic attack on the Bible was repelled, the *Christian Advocate* did not overlook the greater threat to be found in demands for state support for their parochial schools. The *Christian Advocate* declared that, rather than see that Catholic demand satisfied, the Methodists would prefer the destruction of the whole school system of the state.

> No; willingly as they now pay the tax for the support of public schools, and though the institution is of Protestant origin, they would sooner forego all its advantages, and abolish the system, than contribute a cent toward the perpetuation and propagation of a superstition which they believe destructive of religious liberty;

---

[26] *Ibid.*, p. 410. That Bishop Janes did not press his proposal is indicated by the fact that his biography, by Henry B. Ridgway (New York: Phillips and Hunt, 1882), makes no mention of the topic.

[27] *Christian Advocate*, April 24, 1840. In this connection, it is interesting to note that Duvall, *op. cit.*, p. 80, found but two Methodist schools offering courses in the Bible before the Civil War.

[28] *Christian Advocate*, April 24, 1840.

and what is of more fearful consequence, dangerous to the eternal interests of men.[29]

In 1842 the *Christian Advocate* printed a series of articles in defense of the state schools, under the title of "The Common Schools, the Antidote of Jesuitism." The articles discovered a Catholic plot to seize control of the schools of the state. The magazine viewed the prospect with a horrified eye. "We would as soon pass our children through the fire to Moloch, as to commit them to the teaching of Romanist priests."[30] The *Christian Advocate* even found matter for complaint in the celibacy of Catholic priests and nuns, inasmuch as their single state gave the Catholic Church an unfair economic advantage in the financing of schools. "The only possible means of counteracting this advantage is found in public schools; and hence the crafty opposition of the Jesuits to those wise and benevolent institutions."[31]

The *Christian Advocate* applauded the state schools as the best weapon to offset the Catholic threat to American and Protestant liberties. Consequently it was not at all surprised that "the Jesuits, the most devoted of all the monkish orders, should hate the common schools, while Protestants look to them as the sheet anchors of their safety, and the best means of defending [sic] the grand effort now making to bring these United States under the ecclesiastical domination of the Roman pontiff."[32]

The tocsin sounded by the *Christian Advocate* awoke echoes in the *Methodist Quarterly Review*. This chief Methodist quarterly not only supported the thesis that the control of popular elementary education belonged to the state, but even made the then novel proposal that attendance at these state schools be

---

[29] *Ibid.*, February 16, 1842.
[30] *Ibid.*, October 12, 1842.
[31] *Ibid.*, October 5, 1842.
[32] *Ibid.*, October 12, 1842. See also the issues for November 9, 1842 and May 24, 1843.

made compulsory.[33] A later article, however, while opposing public grants to "these ghostly priests for the propagation of the Romish religion,"[34] warned its readers not to rely on the broken reed of state primary schools. It thought it advisable to repeat the warning.

> In our opinion, elementary education has, by far, less power to secure human reason from error than Americans are willing to grant it; and in this particular business of religion, its power is very little indeed, or nothing at all. Look at the delusions of Millerism and Mormonism, at the pestilential heresy of Universalism, &c., if you want proof of it. Besides, this education is fallen already to a great extent into the hands of Rome; and the larger share of it may fall into the same hands hereafter. What then?[35]

Obviously there was increasing interest in Wesleyan circles in the problems of elementary education. This was reflected in the address of the bishops to the General Conference of 1844, which urged the retention of the Bible in the schools of the state.[36] At the same conference a motion was introduced, but not acted upon, that each minister should endeavor to influence the appointment of teachers to the local school.[37]

But questions more pressing than that of Methodist influence on public education engaged the attention of the Wesleyans.

The barbed problem of slavery, which in the forties tore huge rents in the fabric of the Methodist Episcopal Church, left little occasion for discussions of the problem of popular elementary education in Methodist publications. The efforts of the Presbyterians to create parochial schools received but passing mention. The *Christian Advocate* did approve the endeavor, and actually called upon the Methodists to follow the Presbyterian

---

[33] *Methodist Quarterly Review*, XXV (1843), pp. 592 ff.
[34] *Ibid.*, XXVI (1844), p. 360.
[35] *Ibid.*, XXVII (1845), p. 94.
[36] *Journal of General Conference, 1844*, p. 169.
[37] *Ibid.*, p. 88.

example,[38] but this appeal for Methodist parochial schools stirred up no appreciable interest.

In the decade of the fifties, however, the Methodist organs of opinion paid more interest to the problem of popular elementary education. This interest was engendered by the continuing Catholic requests for public funds for their parochial schools.

When the Episcopalian weekly, the *Churchman*, published an appeal by Archbishop Hughes for denominational schools supported by state funds and editorially regretted that church schools were deprived of public funds, the *Christian Advocate* expressed strong disapproval. It commended the state schools and declared that "the new *coalision* [sic] of Romanist and High-Church influence will not be able to shake that system from its foundation."[39]

Nor did the Methodist magazines neglect the propaganda device of reserving the adjectives "American" and "Protestant" for the schools of the state, with the consequent implication that all private and parochial schools were anti-American and anti-Protestant. This device appeared in the *Christian Advocate*, where the Catholic Church is depicted as the irreconciliable enemy of the "American" schools.[40] The *Christian Advocate*, on the other hand, found these schools to be "the pride of our state and the envy of nations, in which Protestantism rejoices."[41]

The *Methodist Quarterly Review* was in agreement with this point of view, and saw in the common schools a marvelous means to transform alien children into good Americans, if not good Protestants.[42] Not only should the American governments

---

[38] *Christian Advocate*, July 5, 1849. In his autobiography, the *Life and Times of George Peck* (New York: Nelson and Phillips, 1874), the editor of the *Advocate* does not consider this unusual appeal worthy of mention.

[39] *Christian Advocate*, December 18, 1851.

[40] *Ibid.*, August 26, 1852.

[41] *Loc. cit.*

[42] *Methodist Quarterly Review*, XXXV (1853), pp. 440 ff.

provide the means to give every immigrant child a Christian education, the magazine declared, but they should use every inducement to get the child into the common school.

The proposal to give an American education to all alien children was seconded by the *Christian Advocate*; and to be sure that this education was truly American, the weekly would allow no voice in the public schools to the Catholic hierarchy.[43]

Later the question of the common schools and Catholicism again engaged the attention of the *Methodist Quarterly Review*. The position taken in the article was the one now commonly assumed by the Methodist press. "Free schools, free presses, free Bibles, free speech and free thought are the natural support of the great principle of Protestantism, which is the right of private judgment in matters of faith and conscience, and these, therefore, must in some way be subjected to Rome's regulating power."[44] The quarterly was not one to tolerate this regulating power. It condemned what it considered an effort on the part of Catholics to break down the system of state schools, an effort which it attributed to the fact that the common schools were incompatible with Roman Catholic interests.

The *Review* also advanced the idea, then new to Methodist publications, that neither the state schools, nor indeed any elementary school, should teach religion. "The day schools, whether public or private, cannot teach religion; they are not meant to do it; and whatever attention the best of them pay to the subject is always superficial and perfunctory."[45]

Towards the end of the decade of the fifties the highest courts of Methodism reflected the interest of the Wesleyan publications in the problem of elementary education. In 1856 the General Conference of the Methodist Church, now without dele-

---

[43] *Christian Advocate,* June 16, 1853.
[44] *Methodist Quarterly Review,* XXXIX (1857), p. 36.
[45] *Ibid.,* p. 524.

gates from the slave states, listened to a report of its Committee
on Education which discussed the subject.[46] The committee asked
the General Conference to foster an increased Wesleyan influence on the schools of the state. It noted the unsatisfied demand
for common-school teachers and suggested the establishment of
Methodist normal schools to supply this demand. It declared it
to be the duty of the Methodists "to feel a deep concern for the
common schools and academies of our country,"[47] but it would
not have this Methodist concern shown openly. "Our agency in
this respect should be employed prudently, and in such a man-
ner as to show that we have no selfish or sectarian end in view,
but merely desire to do our share in the great work of educating
the nation."[48]

After their withdrawal from the Methodist Church the southern Methodists had created the Methodist Episcopal Church,
South, and formed their own General Conference. The first meetings of this new conference did not discuss the question of popular elementary education; but since in the slave states which it
represented state school systems were not yet flourishing, the
need of primary schools was of more pressing importance to the
southern Methodists than to the northern. This need was manifested by the creation by southern Wesleyans of an Educational
Institute, which held several meetings. The fruit of these meetings was a number of resolutions which were presented to the
southern General Conference of 1858.[49] As a result of this activity the Committee on Education of the General Conference
handed in a report which urged the propriety of establishing

---

[46] *Journal of General Conference, 1856*, p. 308.

[47] *Loc. cit.*

[48] *Loc. cit. Journal of General Conference, 1860*, p. 463, shows that the northern
Methodists had 103 secondary schools with 21,616 pupils, and no primary
schools.

[49] *Methodist Episcopal Church, South, Journal of General Conference, 1858*, p. 436.
The journal does not give the actual resolutions.

Methodist elementary schools.[50] It demanded that all Methodist congregations should survey their localities to determine the practicability of these schools, and, "if found feasible, to take immediate steps to accomplish" their establishment.[51]

This move of the southern Committee on Education, unique in the histories of the General Conferences of the Methodist churches, is explained by the lack of schools in the slave states. Where the state did not act, the Methodist Church would. It would not appear that the Methodist Church was reviving the traditional claim of the Christian Church to control popular elementary education. It seems more likely that southern Methodists were endeavoring to fulfill a function which they recognized as belonging properly to the state. Nor did this movement among the southern Methodists ever develop. It was laid aside necessarily during the Civil War, and never taken up again. When the General Conference of the southern Methodists next assembled in 1866, educational questions were largely ignored. Although the southern Methodists later discussed secondary education, never again did they consider the establishment of Methodist elementary schools.

Until the end of the Civil War problems concerned with that irrepressible conflict engrossed the attention of the Wesleyan periodicals and assemblies of the North. During those bitter years the question of popular education did not seem to be of major importance, yet the topic came up at the meeting of the General Conference in 1864. A motion was introduced that the Committee on Education be instructed to study the relation of the Methodist Church to popular education.[52] The committee was also requested to suggest measures which would enable the Wesleyans "to secure our proportionate influence and control

---

[50] *Ibid.*, p. 533.
[51] *Loc. cit.*
[52] *Journal of General Conference, 1864*, p. 110.

in the management and instruction" in the schools of the state.[53] While the General Conference adopted the resolution, nothing further was recorded about the matter.

A few years after the Civil War the *Christian Advocate* rediscovered the Catholic threat to the public schools. The fireworks were touched off by its discovery of the grant of public funds to parochial schools in New York. In opposing this Catholic "attack" the *Christian Advocate* defended the common schools as "not only not 'godless,' but positively moral and religious in their influence."[54] It hailed the public school as the "chief pillar, next to the Church of God, upon which securely reposes a republican government—the American system of public school education."[55] It went on to demand that the state schools should be secularized. "It is not through indifference to religion, but through conscientious interest for it, that the Protestantism of this country would restrict the common school system to purely literary and scientific instruction."[56] For several years the *Christian Advocate* sounded the tocsin again and again.[57]

Late in 1871 a convention of New York Methodists adopted a resolution condemning the grant of public money to church schools, and petitioned the New York Legislature to amend the State Constitution to ban such grants.[58] Rather surprisingly, the *Christian Advocate* raised its voice against the proposed amendment.[59] The magazine reaffirmed its strong approval of the state schools; but, it went on to say, if private or parochial schools

---

[53] *Loc. cit.*
[54] *Christian Advocate*, March 4, 1869.
[55] *Loc. cit.*
[56] *Ibid.*, June 3, 1869.
[57] *Ibid.*, March 4, June 3, June 10, November 25, 1869; January 13, March 17, April 14, September 15, 1870; March 2, March 16, March 23, November 16, 1871.
[58] *Ibid.*, December 28, 1871.
[59] *Loc. cit.*

may co-exist with public schools without adversely affecting state education, they should be tolerated. If the church schools supplement the work of the state schools, "we cannot see why they may not receive a share of the public funds."[60] This was a new departure in a Methodist magazine.

Then the *Christian Advocate,* after thinking over the matter for a few weeks, announced a three-point policy on the question of popular elementary education.

> 1. That our common schools are a public necessity, and should be maintained by the State; and that all the children of the State should be required to attend them.
>
> 2. That they should be, as public schools, purely secular, observing no religious forms, except by common consent, and imposing no religious lessons.
>
> 3. That no rival schools, by which the efficiency of the common schools would be interfered with, should be allowed; though the aid of such schools might be accepted when needed for the public necessities, and then such should be compensated by the State.[61]

To this policy the *Christian Advocate* adhered in subsequent issues.[62] A like point of view was adopted by the *Methodist Quarterly Review.*[63]

Thus did the official publications of the Methodist Episcopal Church formulate an answer to the question of the control of popular primary education. Where the state has not yet provided adequate facilities, the church may be allowed to conduct elementary schools, not as a matter of right, but only as a concession of the state. The state, and the state alone, has the right to control popular elementary education. From the principle that popular education belongs entirely and exclusively to the

---

[60] *Loc. cit.*

[61] *Ibid.,* January 25, 1872.

[62] *Ibid.,* March 7, March 21, 1872; April 1, May 15, 1875.

[63] *Methodist Quarterly Review,* LVI (1874), pp. 181-213, 522-44; LXIII (1881), pp. 635-64. For a slightly different viewpoint see LXII (1880), pp. 299-315.

state, the *Christian Advocate* explicitly and quite logically drew two important corollaries. All elementary education should be secular, and this secularized state education should be imposed on all children.

The oft-voiced concern of the *Christian Advocate* about the Catholic Church and its relations with the schools of the state was reflected in the General Conference of the Methodist Church of 1872. In their address to the delegates the bench of bishops warned the Methodist Church that "the combined and persistent efforts making [sic] by the bishops and priests of the Romish Church to destroy our system of common schools attract much public attention."[64] They championed the state schools, and declared that American civil and religious liberty demand a virtuous and educated populace.

> It becomes us, therefore, cordially to unite with all intelligent Christians and all true patriots to cherish the free institutions bequeathed us by our Protestant forefathers, in giving an intelligent, firm and earnest support to the civil authorities in maintaining, extending and rendering more efficient our system of primary education, until all the people throughout the land shall share in its benefits and participate in its blessings.[65]

The General Conference, inspired by this address of the Methodist bishops, formally adopted the following preambles and resolutions.

> Whereas, We have always, as a Church, accepted the work of education as a duty enjoined by our commission to "teach all nations"; and
> Whereas, The system of Common Schools is an indispensible safeguard to republican institutions; and
> Whereas, The combined and persistent assaults of the Romanists and others endanger the very existence of our Common Schools; therefore,

---

[64] *Journal of General Conference, 1872,* p. 456.
[65] *Loc. cit.*

Resolved, 1. That we will cooperate in every effort which is fitted to make our Common Schools more efficient and permanent.

Resolved, 2. That it is our firm conviction that to divide the common school funds among religious denominations for educational purposes is wrong in principle and hostile to our free institutions and the cause of education.

Resolved, 3. That we will resist all means which may be employed to exclude from the Common Schools the Bible, which is the charter of our liberties and the inspiration of our civilization.[66]

In these preambles and resolutions the Methodist Episcopal Church paradoxically asserted at one and the same time that the Methodist Church has an obligation to teach, and that it should not teach. The Wesleyan Church obviously had no intention of establishing church primary schools. It found that it fulfilled its function as teacher by officially approving the schools of the state. The obligation of the church to teach is further satisfied if it sees to it that the Bible is retained in the schools of the state. The duty of the church to teach is still further exercised by condemning the efforts of another Christian church to obtain support for its elementary schools.

Thus did the supreme governing body of the Methodist Episcopal Church officially interpret the traditional claim of the Christian Church to control popular primary education. Summarily, it rejected that claim. The action of the General Conference, like the views of the official Methodist publications, was not determined by any well-considered Christian philosophy of education. The Methodist stand on the control of popular elementary education was assumed simply as a reaction to the position of the Catholic Church.

Subsequent articles in the *Methodist Quarterly Review* reaffirmed the position of the General Conference of 1872.[67] In the magazine appeared a report made to the New York City

---

[66] *Ibid.*, p. 44.
[67] *Methodist Quarterly Review*, LVI (1874), pp. 181 ff., 519 ff.

Council of Political Reform by Dexter A. Hawkins on the topic
of compulsory education. So important did the editors of the
Methodist quarterly consider the document that they published
it in a special, indeed a unique, supplement to their magazine,
with an introductory note stating that it deserved "the careful
study of every American citizen."[68]

The report declared that "those unerring guides of the statesman—statistics" prove that universal education leads to universal morality.[69] Hawkins finds that universal education tends
to universal morality only if the state conducts the schools. Indeed, a large part of his report is devoted to an effort to prove
that "the parochial school system produces more illiterates,
paupers, and criminals than ours."[70] The parochial schools he
had in mind were those of the Catholic Church, which he de-
scribes in strong language. A priori, it would be difficult to see
how schools explicitly Christian are more inimical to morals
than schools specifically secular; but with the aid of those unerring guides of the statesman, statistics, Hawkins concluded
that to teach religion is to train criminals.

The noteworthy fact about this attack on the right of a Christian church to control popular elementary education was its
publication in an official periodical of the Methodist Church. It
may be taken as the terminal point of the evolution of Methodist
opinion on the control of that education. By their words and
actions Wesley and Asbury had insisted on the traditional claim
of the church to exercise control over popular education. Less
than a century after the death of its founders, the American
Methodist Church had repudiated that claim.

Nor was the Methodist Church content to surrender only for
itself the traditional claim of the Christian Church to control

---

[68] *Vol. cit.*, Supplement, p. 1.
[69] *Ibid.*, p. 6.
[70] *Ibid.*, pp. 10 ff.

popular elementary education. From its premises it quite logically deduced that, if the Methodist Church had no voice in the
control of primary education, no Christian church had a valid
claim in that field. Most expressions on the subject in the official
Methodist periodicals were vocalizations of this deduction. These
magazines not only demanded universal compulsory education
in the state schools, but even attacked the right of a Christian
church to conduct its own schools.

Unavoidable is the conclusion that the major factor in the
Methodist rejection of the ancient claim of the Christian Church
to control primary education was animus against Catholicism.

CHAPTER VII

The
Baptists

The congregational polity of the Baptists confronts the historian with such difficulties that even Baptist chroniclers have been loath to attempt general histories of that denomination in the United States. There were, in 1942, over 63,000 Baptist congregations in America.[1] While some of these maintained complete independence, most were organized—if "organized" is the word—into very loose associations numbering into the hundreds. At first glance, it would appear fortunate that most Baptist associations maintained relations with four major national Baptist conventions. Since these conventions have been, if possible, even more loosely organized than the local associations, the historian finds little help here.

A large proportion of American Baptists are Negroes; two thirds of all American Negroes who are members of churches belong, it is estimated, to Baptist congregations.[2] Most of these local churches are members of two conventions, both claiming the title of National Baptist Convention, and neither established

---

[1] Benson Y. Landis, editor, *Yearbook of American Churches, 1943*, p. 148. Lebanon: Sowers Printing Company, 1943.
[2] Willard L. Sperry, *Religion in America*, p. 288. New York: The Macmillan Company, 1946.

before the closing decades of the nineteenth century. Passing references to these Negro groups are made in the general Baptist histories, but no noteworthy attempt has been made to recount their story. It can safely be assumed that these Negro Baptists had little to do with forming Protestant opinion on the question of the control of popular elementary education. More important is the history of the white Baptist congregations, but the few general histories which cover their development do not touch upon the relations of the Baptists to popular primary education.[3]

At the beginning of the nineteenth century American Baptists developed an interest in the work of foreign missions. This interest brought about the establishment, in 1814, of a loose national organization. The question of slavery wrecked this group in 1844. Its northern members kept this association in existence. It is with the educational philosophy of this group, now known as the American Baptist Convention, that the present study is concerned.

The southern schismatics created, in 1845, the fourth major national Baptist association, the Southern Baptist Convention. A recent doctoral dissertation on the history of education within this faction shows that the Southern Baptist Convention not only did not create Baptist elementary schools, but never seriously considered the problem of the control of popular primary education during the nineteenth century.[4] The state had assumed

---

[3] See Albert H. Newman, editor, *A Century of Baptist Achievement* (Philadelphia: American Baptist Publication Society, 1901), and his *History of the Baptist Churches in the United States,* sixth edition revised and enlarged (Philadelphia: American Baptist Publication Society, 1915) ; John T. Christian, *History of the Baptists* (Nashville: Sunday School Board of the Southern Baptist Convention, 1922) ; Henry C. Vedder, *The Baptists* (New York: Baker and Taylor Company, 1903), *History of the Baptists in the Middle States* (Philadelphia: American Baptist Publication Society, 1898), *Short History of the Baptists* (Philadelphia: American Baptist Publication Society, 1907).

[4] Edith C. Magruder, *A Historical Study of the Educational Agencies of the Southern Baptist Convention, 1845-1945.* New York: Teachers College, Columbia University, 1951.

the control of popular education; the southern Baptists never questioned its right.

In the days before the achievement of American independence the Baptists were somewhat concerned about education. They were instrumental in establishing a number of schools, chief among which is the present Brown University; nor did they neglect efforts to create Latin grammar schools, as well as schools of lower grade.[5]

In the early nineteenth century the educational question which most exercised the Baptists was the theological training of ministers. Important elements within the Baptist Church were bitterly opposed to theological seminaries.[6] It is uncertain whether the opposition of these elements, usually known as "hard-shell" or "landmarker" Baptists, influenced to any great extent Baptist views on education in general. Nevertheless it would appear that the Baptists, as late as the fourth decade of the nineteenth century, were, in the words of a Baptist historian, "far from being interested in general education."[7] Nor were they even greatly concerned over the question of religious education in the schools of the state; a historian declares that the Baptist reaction to the problem, "while not one of total indifference, was characterized by an attitude of comparative passivity."[8] There is some little evidence that Baptists wished to promote elementary education on the frontier as part of their missionary endeavor;[9] but this evidence is slight, certainly too small to support the suggestion that the Baptists deliberately

---

[5] Carl B. Wilson, *The Baptist Manual Labor School Movement*, p. 18. Waco: Baylor University Press, 1937.

[6] Newman, *History of the Baptist Churches in the United States*, p. 380, declares: "The mass of the Baptists were indifferent or hostile to ministerial education."

[7] Frank G. Lewis, *A Sketch of the History of Baptist Education in Pennsylvania*, p. 20. Chester: Crozer Theological Seminary, 1919.

[8] Bell, *op. cit.*, p. 209.

[9] William W. Sweet, editor, *Religion on the American Frontier*, I, p. 64. 4 vols., Chicago: University of Chicago Press, 1931-1946.

chose to expend their resources on the education of the frontier rather than on the primary education of their own children.[10] The Baptists never made that choice.

The Baptists in the state of Horace Mann obviously would be among the first Baptist groups to react to the movement for popular elementary education led by the Massachusetts educational statesman. Towards the end of the 1830's the Boston *Watchman*, one of the most influential of the Baptist weeklies, published several articles in praise of the common schools, which showed that the *Watchman* had already accepted the thesis that the state had the right to control popular elementary education.[11] Indeed, the magazine, even at that early date, considered with equanimity the idea of compulsory education of all children in the state schools.[12]

The leading Baptist quarterly, the *Christian Review*, gave its approval to the efforts of the state to impart rudimentary education.[13] It expressed a desire that the state schools teach religion; but it found that dogmatic instruction was less important in the common than in the higher schools.[14] It would appear that the *Christian Review* was ready to distinguish between secular primary education under state control and religious higher education conducted by the church, a distinction that was soon to be made.

-----

[10] This thesis is implied in Wilson, *op. cit.*, p. 47: "There are numerous accounts to show that the Baptists were for the most part interested in a democratic system of education. They were, however, as a body, very poor, and knew that it would be impossible to sustain their missionary program as it should be administered, and at the same time make adequate provision for all the children of the denomination." The author gives no evidence to support this contention, nor has the present writer seen any.

[11] *Watchman*, February 3, February 10, February 17, 1837; August 23, 1839; October 16, 1840.

[12] *Ibid.*, February 3, February 10, 1837.

[13] *Christian Review*, V (1840), pp. 218-29, 396-418; VI (1841), pp. 1-29; VIII (1843), pp. 514-21.

[14] *Ibid.*, VI (1841), p. 25.

The *Watchman* did not overlook Catholic efforts to obtain public funds in New York City.[15] By way of advice to Catholics it declared:

> If the children of Papists are really in danger of being corrupted in the Protestant schools of enlightened, free and happy America, it may be well for their *conscientious* parents and still more *conscientious priests*, to return them to the privileges of their ancestral homes, among the half-tamed boors of Germany, the swarming lazzaroni of Italy, or the ragged, turf-sheltered, sans-potatoe [*sic*] peasantry of the Emerald Isle.[16]

Apart from the colorful language, the noteworthy element in this effusion is the Baptist belief that the common schools were Protestant institutions.

Nor did events nearer home escape the *Watchman*. It expressed its "deep regret" over the opening of a Catholic school; "it is an injustice to those children who are hereafter to claim the rights of American citizens."[17] Here is an early intimation that a church school is somehow un-American, a charge later to be made explicit.

Baptist periodicals early debated the secularization of elementary education. In 1843 the *Watchman* approved religious instruction in the state schools; it found no difficulty about dogmatic instruction in the secondary schools, for these should be conducted by the churches.[18] In the following year the magazine changed its position, and declared that it was "not desirable to teach the doctrines of grace in the public schools."[19] A few years later, however, the *Watchman* once more changed its mind. After sounding the praises of public education,[20] it discussed "Sec-

---

15 *Watchman*, June 25, November 5, December 10, 1841; January 21, April 1, 1842.
16 *Ibid.*, June 25, 1841.
17 *Ibid.*, January 13, 1843.
18 *Ibid.*, August 4, 1843.
19 *Ibid.*, November 22, 1844. See also November 29, December 13, 1844.
20 *Ibid.*, January 17, February 21, March 7, March 14, 1850.

tarianism and the Public Schools."[21] Although it discovered a
papal plot to destroy the common schools, the weekly approved
church schools: "Sectarian institutions, supported by private
munificence, are not objectionable; on the contrary we deem
them necessary and proper."[22] In the indispensable common
schools "the great principles of Christianity, in which all agree,
should be as faithfully inculcated as the dogmas of a sect are
religiously excluded."[23]

At the same time the columns of the *Examiner* contained a
debate occasioned by the proposed free-school law pending before the New York Legislature.[24] Most of the contributors approved the proposed law; several found that a good reason to
support the law was that the Catholics were reputedly opposed
to it. This Catholic opposition was declared to be "a device of
the Man of Sin to keep the masses in ignorance and thereby
make them dupes of a secular priesthood, to overthrow our free
institutions."[25] One of the opponents of the law felt compelled
to object that it was "impolitic and unjust in the extreme to support an unjust and oppressive law merely because a particular
religious sect is opposed to it."[26]

The *Watchman,* from the distance of Boston, did not engage
in the debate; but it gave editorial praise to the proposed law.[27]
Extending its horizons even further, it spoke in praise of pro-
posals made in England for the establishment there of a free,
tax-supported nonsectarian system of schools under the control
of the state.[28] Coming closer to home, it once more highly

---

[21] *Ibid.,* May 9, 1850.
[22] *Loc. cit.*
[23] *Loc. cit.*
[24] *Examiner,* August 8, September 5, September 12, October 3, October 24, 1850.
[25] *Ibid.,* August 8, 1850. The term "Man of Sin" was a name frequently applied to
    the pope.
[26] *Ibid.,* October 24, 1850.
[27] *Watchman,* January 30, 1851.
[28] *Ibid.,* February 15, 1851.

praised the common schools of Massachusetts.[29] Its expressions of approval were seconded by the *Christian Review;* that magazine was pleased to find that the state schools were still Christian institutions.[30]

The *Christian Review* also shared the concern being manifested by the *Watchman* at the Catholic threat to the common schools.[31] The quarterly devoted a rather lengthy article to the question.[32] Lamenting the expulsion of the Bible from the public schools of New York, it rejoiced that the state schools in New England were still Protestant, "inasmuch as the Bible still has a place in them."[33] The *Review* conceded the Catholics the right to conduct schools; "but all thinking men, who are free from the prejudices of which the Romanists are unfortunately the subjects, must look on such a measure as fraught with great evil."[34] The magazine demanded that the public schools teach a minimum religious course agreeable to all denominations. It made its own the words of Horace Bushnell: "We can take the ground explicitly, and clear of all ambiguity, that those who exclude themselves [from the common schools] are not Americans, and are not acting in their complaints or agitations on any principle that meets the tenor of our American institutions."[35] Thus the leading Baptist quarterly asserted its belief that those Christians who maintained the traditional claim of the church to control popular elementary education were un-American.

The interest of Baptist periodicals in education during the early years of the 1850's was reflected in the most popular Bap-

---

29 *Ibid.,* February 29, 1851.
30 *Christian Review,* XVI (1851), p. 278.
31 *Watchman,* April 7, April 21, April 28, May 5, 1853.
32 *Christian Review,* XVIII (1853), pp. 441-58.
33 *Ibid.,* p. 446.
34 *Ibid.,* p. 450.
35 *Ibid.,* p. 455. For Bushnell's opposition to the Catholic schools see George Stewart, *History of Religious Education in Connecticut to 1850,* pp. 287 ff. (New Haven: Yale University Press, 1924).

tist monthly, *Ford's Christian Repository*. Besides several articles on female and ministerial education,[36] that magazine, in
1853, published two articles urging the spread of popular education in the states of the South.[37] Thereafter the monthly maintained silence on the subject until its suspension at the outbreak
of the Civil War; and this silence was continued after the magazine was revived in the 1870's.

Nor did the columns of the *Examiner* show much interest in
education until several years of peace had followed Appomattox.
A few articles did appear, approving the education of the freed-
men,[38] lauding the New York public schools,[39] and opposing, on
the grounds that education was a local affair, the proposed
United States Bureau of Education.[40] The *Examiner* forgot its
detachment when, towards the end of 1868, it rediscovered the
Catholic threat to the state schools. Thereupon the weekly un-
leashed a spate of articles on the question.[41]

One of the articles is noteworthy for its expression of the
Examiner's belief that the state schools were Protestant schools,
and schools inimical to Catholicism.

> The Pope hates our free schools, because they comprise one of the
> strong barriers against his schemes which Protestantism has reared
> for the defense of freedom.
>
> Indirectly, our free schools are Protestant agencies; and they
> are so, because in enlightening his mind, they enable the Catholic
> youth to see through the false and unreasonable assumption of the
> "infallible Pope." First the teaching is distrusted, then the teacher;

---

[36] *Ford's Christian Repository*, I (1852), pp. 501-06; II (1853), pp. 30-40, 67-72;
IV (1855), pp. 529-34.
[37] *Ibid.*, II (1853), pp. 337-38, 377-91.
[38] *Examiner*, April 18, 1867.
[39] *Ibid.*, March 7, 1867; February 13, March 5, 1868.
[40] *Ibid.*, February 20, 1868.
[41] *Ibid.*, December 10, 1868; April 1, May 20, July 29, September 30, November 11,
November 18, December 23, 1869; February 3, March 31, April 14, May 5,
1870; January 4, February 15, February 29, 1872.

and herein do they constitute one of the great safeguards of the Republic which is founded on Protestant principles, against the aggressions of the Papacy.[42]

Fear of the Catholic threat to the schools of the state also stirred the *Examiner* to consider some other educational problems. It reversed its condemnation of a federal Bureau of Education, and approved the suggestion that the control of popular elementary education be vested in the national rather than in the state governments.[43] It also placed the editorial stamp of approval on the proposal to make education compulsory.[44]

Interesting was the opinion it expressed on the control of secondary education. It maintained in several articles that, while elementary education should be secular, the colleges should be religious.[45] Its main argument was based on the contention that, for a true and complete education, the student must imbibe a Christian atmosphere. The pupils of the elementary schools lived with their families; consequently the purely secular education given by the state schools was remedied by the Christian atmosphere of the home. The majority of the college students, on the contrary, were boarders at their schools. The colleges therefore are bound to create a Christian atmosphere within their walls; and the colleges could do this only if they were church institutions.

The *Watchman*, too, continued its interest in the problems of education. While it discussed the problem of the national control of education[46] and urged the Baptists to establish more and better academies,[47] its main concern was about the Catholic threat. It approved resolutions condemning the grant of public

---

[42] *Ibid.*, March 31, 1870.
[43] *Ibid.*, May 5, 1870.
[44] *Ibid.*, November 24, 1870.
[45] *Ibid.*, July 22, October 7, 1869.
[46] *Watchman*, April 7, 1870.
[47] *Ibid.*, May 5, 1870.

funds to sectarian schools.[48] It demanded the retention of Holy Writ in the public schools; "if our nation stands, it must be on Bible truth."[49] It found justification for the state to close the doors of all schools controlled by the Catholic Church; it declared that the Catholic's

> right to withdraw his child from the public school in order that he may educate it within the Church might perhaps be granted; though we can easily see how the State might well refuse to recognize even this right.
>
> When a father proposes to put his boy into the hands of masters whose alphabet of truth is that the ecclesiastical law or the church canons rule the civil law of the country, a State might be justified in interfering and, taking the boy away from father and masters, placing him under a system less inimical to its own safety.[50]

In 1870 there assembled the first of several national Baptist educational conventions. More than a hundred delegates, representing Baptist education societies and schools in nineteen states, were present. In lieu of more specific statistics, the convention reported that the Baptist denomination conducted several theological seminaries, a large number of colleges, and a few academies; no Baptist elementary schools were discovered.[51]

The question of the control of popular elementary education was considered by the convention. A special committee was created to report on state grants to sectarian schools. The report, which was adopted by the assembly, and which condemned the donation of public money to church schools, affirmed the right of the state to control schools in which rudimentary education

---

[48] *Ibid.*, April 28, 1870.
[49] *Ibid.*, November 17, 1870.
[50] *Ibid.*, February 3, 1870.
[51] *Proceedings of the National Baptist Educational Convention, 1870*, p. 198 (New York: Sheldon and Company, 1870). Vedder, *The Baptists*, p. 200, finds that, while Baptist schools in 1900 had 38,000 students, there were but 2,400 enrolled in Baptist schools in 1870.

was given *gratis*. The concluding resolutions summed up the report of the committee.

> That for the safety of the State as such, the common school is a necessity and ought to be maintained; and that it is unconstitutional and morally wrong for the State to appropriate public money for any ecclesiastical purpose whatever.
>
> That all legislation tending on the one hand to deprive our children of the common school, and on the other to support institutions designed to propagate special forms of denominational belief, is subversive alike of the well-being of the State and of those rights of the individual conscience which arise out of our strictly personal obligations to Almighty God.
>
> That in these resolutions we are simply reaffirming those fundamental principles of religious freedom, which Baptist churches have always sacredly cherished, and what they first, among the religious organizations of Christendom, adopted as articles of faith.[52]

The meetings of the Educational Convention proved of interest to the Baptist periodicals. The *Watchman* expressed satisfaction with the resolutions just cited.[53] The *Examiner* voiced its regrets that the convention had not seen fit to adopt a resolution protesting the exclusion of Sacred Scripture from the common schools of the state.[54] One of the leaders of the convention reviewed its work in the pages of the *Baptist Quarterly*, successor to the now defunct *Christian Review*.[55]

Protestant objections to the grant of state funds to Catholic elementary schools were not always matched by Protestant objections to the grant of state funds to Protestant secondary schools. This understandable anomaly attracted the attention of the *Watchman*. In an editorial rather formidably entitled "Church and State," the weekly enunciated what it termed Bap-

---

[52] *Proceedings*, p. 249.
[53] *Watchman*, April 28, 1870.
[54] *Examiner*, May 5, 1870.
[55] *Baptist Quarterly*, V (1871), pp. 206-29.

tist principles.[56] It declared that Christ's kingdom is not of this world. It asserted that "civil government—we write from an American standpoint—knows nothing about the religious views of its people." It found that, since the government could possess no property save that entrusted to it by the people, grants to one sect are robbery of the rest. It stated that many believed there were areas open to the conjoint action of church and state, specifically the area of secondary education, where the state should assist the church by financial gifts. The *Watchman* strongly condemned any such donations: "There is just as much reason why the Church and the State should act together in the lower education as in the higher; and then comes the end of our common school system and the return of the petty parochial schools of a darker age."[57]

The question of the secularization of public education would not down. The Baptists usually saw this problem in simple terms of "the Bible in the schools." The Reverend Alvah Hovey, in an article in the *Examiner*, found the Bible to be a sectarian book which should be banned from the state schools.[58] A contributor to the *Baptist Quarterly*, on the other hand, found that an essential principle of America is Christianity, which is defined as "the authority of the Bible as the revelation of God."[59] "The Bible is the constitution of our constitution and our subfundamental law."[60] That subfundamental law should be "the chief subject of public instruction."[61] In his zeal for the Bible in the schools the author abandoned the Protestant right of private judgment to the state; "and the extent and minuteness with which the State shall teach the religion which happens actually

---

56 *Watchman*, April 27, 1871.
57 *Loc. cit.*
58 *Examiner*, June 21, 1871.
59 *Baptist Quarterly*, V (1871), p. 277.
60 *Ibid.*, p. 284.
61 *Ibid.*, p. 285.

to be at the bottom of its existence is a matter for itself to determine."[62] Hovey, however, used the columns of the *Baptist Quarterly* to reaffirm his position.[63]

The Second National Baptist Educational Convention assembled in 1872, with representatives from twenty-two states.
The Baptist rejection of church control of elementary education
was underlined in the creation by the convention of a special
committee significantly entitled "On Academies as the Base of
Denominational Institutions of Learning."[64] The Baptists would
not even consider Baptist primary schools.

As an appointed part of the proceedings an address, given
by the Reverend Barnas Sears, discussed the question of church
control of elementary education. The speaker declared that the
function of religious instruction should be exercised by the
home, the church, and the Sunday school. It did not follow,
however, that the state schools should be secular; they must be
Christian. "Wherever both teacher and pupil attempt to follow
the golden rule, and the Lord's Prayer and David's psalms of
praise are repeated daily, there the best schools will be found."[65]
The instant that doctrinal instruction is attempted, as in church-
controlled schools, the best school is ruined; "the moment sectarian instruction is introduced, the good effect ceases and evil
enters."[66] Consequently the speaker repudiated the suggestion
that the control of popular primary education should be trans-
ferred from the hands of the state to the church or private
groups. "General education must be provided not only for the
people, but through the people."[67]

---

[62] *Ibid.*, p. 287.
[63] *Ibid.*, VI (1872), pp. 42-51.
[64] *Proceedings of the National Baptist Educational Convention, 1872*, p. 45. New
    York: Sheldon and Company, 1872.
[65] *Ibid.*, p. 16.
[66] *Loc. cit.*
[67] *Ibid.*, p. 18.

Two editorials in the *Watchman,* each with the title "Denominational Schools," show the dichotomy of Baptist thought in the estimation of Baptist and of Catholic endeavors to conduct schools. The first is an ardent defense, against the objections of the secularists, of the Baptist Church's right to conduct its own schools for the training of good Baptists.[68] The second is an attack on the exercise of the same right by the Catholic Church.[69] The magazine declared that only if the people of a state were of one religion, "a close connection between education and religion would be desirable."[70] It condemned sectarian schools, because such schools fostered religious animosities. It found, as a special reason for approving the state schools, the fact that many defections from the Catholic Church occurred, "and to the common school system this result is due rather than to any other cause."[71] The magazine was not content to sound the alarm about the Catholic threat to the state schools; it warned that the Catholic hierarchy plotted to seize control of the United States: "to such a scheme our common-school system is the most formidable obstacle, and its abolition is the first step in the scheme of conquest—conquest by the porcine virtue of fertility."[72] Evidently the *Watchman* believed that the divine command to increase and multiply did not apply to Catholics.

Shortly thereafter the *Watchman* threw its support to the proposal of compulsory education by the state.[73] It supported its position by references to the report on compulsory education by Dexter Hawkins, which found that parochial schools produced more criminals, paupers, and illiterates than state schools.[74]

---

[68] *Watchman,* February 27, 1873.
[69] *Ibid.,* February 19, 1874.
[70] *Loc. cit.*
[71] *Loc. cit.*
[72] *Loc. cit.*
[73] *Ibid.,* May 7, 1874.
[74] For a discussion of Hawkins' report see Chapter VI, "The Methodists," *ad finem.*

The *Baptist Quarterly* in 1874 turned to the question of the control of secondary education.[75] Taking for granted state control of elementary education, it sought to extend that control to secondary schools. To justify state colleges the article could find but one reason: since the state had the right to control primary education, it also had the right to prepare the teachers to impart this elementary instruction. Since an apparently adequate supply of teachers was coming from private and church colleges, the article was momentarily baffled in its endeavor to extend state control of education, but it triumphantly came up with an artful solution. "As a *hopeful experiment,* then, the State is justified in appropriating money for higher education, with the view of promoting thereby the instruction of all the youth of the country."[76]

Now that it had justified the entrance of the state into the field of higher education, the magazine considered the question of religious instruction in these secondary institutions of the state. Since in secondary schools, in contradistinction to primary schools, religious education is necessary, the state, it asserted, might find itself compelled to teach dogmatics—not, however, to strengthen the church, but to sustain the state; this education in religion, however, should not be "sectarian."[77]

The Reverend Alvah Hovey once more used the columns of the *Baptist Quarterly* to deny that the state possessed the right of teaching religion in any school.[78] The state had the duty of giving its citizens the rudiments of learning, and nothing more. Non-Protestants should not be offended by the use of the Common Version of the Bible in the state schools; yet while Christian morality should be inculcated in the pupils, that training did not require the custom of Bible reading.

---

[75] *Baptist Quarterly,* VIII (1874), pp. 481-93.
[76] *Ibid.,* p. 484.
[77] *Ibid.,* p. 489.
[78] *Ibid.,* pp. 65-79.

The *Watchman*, discussing "The State and Religion," found occasion to praise Hovey's stand, and set forth its position in a paraphrase of his article.[79]

> 1. There is no sufficient reason why the State should furnish to all the people anything more than the rudiments of education; their religious training properly belongs to parents and Sabbath school teachers.
>
> 2. There is no sufficient reason why the public schools should be made offensive to Jews or Papists, Buddhists or Mohammedans, by enforcing the use of the Common Version of the New Testament.
>
> 3. The morals of Christianity can be taught even in public schools without reading the Bible there. There is no objection to portions of the Bible simply as an English classic.

After again urging its readers to support Baptist academies,[80] the *Watchman* once more returned to the question of the state and education.[81] Reiterating its contention that the state should control only elementary education, it condemned state taxation for the support of secondary education as a levy on the whole people for the special advantage of a few. It rejected the contention that state secondary education would enable the poor to gain an education otherwise out of their reach; for the Christian Church already "provides that the worthy poor shall enjoy out of the Lord's treasury what the rich can obtain for themselves. Christianity has no higher mission in relation to human society than to give the poor the best possible education."[82] It assailed demands on the state to aid the Church in any of its works as "demoralizing in the highest sense—interfering with its highest destiny—the training of independent, self-reliant sons of God."[83]

---

[79] *Watchman*, January 20, 1874.
[80] *Ibid.*, January 29, 1874.
[81] *Ibid.*, February 5, 1874.
[82] *Loc. cit.*
[83] *Loc. cit.*

The *Examiner* joined the *Watchman* in urging its readers to support their Baptist educational institutions.[84] It did not neglect the Catholic threat to the public-school system,[85] but it expressed its disapproval of Grant's message on the state of the Union of 1875, which, *inter alia,* called for the taxation of church schools. It did not, however, condemn the message out of a desire to protect church schools, but because it believed the president of the United States should not interfere in matters concerning local government.[86]

After several articles supporting Baptist secondary schools,[87] the *Baptist Quarterly* examined the relations of the state to education.[88] In primary education the writer advocated universal and compulsory education, which should be "neither Protestant nor Catholic, Theistic nor Atheistic, but simply secular."[89] If the King James Version offends anyone, "better, a thousand times better, the free schools without the Bible than no free schools."[90] While the state should control elementary education, it should leave secondary education to the church. The elementary schools are essential to the existence of the state; the secondary schools are not. State primary schools benefit the whole people; state secondary schools help only the rich. Elementary education can omit religious instruction; secondary education cannot. Since only the church can supply this religious education, the state should leave the church in complete and unchallenged control of secondary education.

In the Baptist congresses held during the eighties the question of religion and education arose. One speaker at the third

---

84 *Examiner,* August 28, October 28, 1875.
85 *Ibid.,* March 25, 1875.
86 *Ibid.,* December 16, 1875.
87 *Baptist Quarterly,* X (1876), pp. 19-28, 445-66.
88 *Ibid.,* XI (1877), pp. 337-51.
89 *Ibid.,* p. 342.
90 *Ibid.,* p. 345.

congress found the Bible in the state schools "next to nothing—not worth fighting for—really accomplishing almost nothing where it is still maintained."[91]

The fifth meeting of the congress, which explicitly discussed religious education in state schools, showed a wide variety of opinions. The first speaker found the Bible in the public schools a violation of the religious liberty of Catholics, and urged his hearers to obtain for the Catholics "what they are too feeble to enforce, immunity from taxation in support of a Protestant establishment."[92] Not only did he condemn all religious exercises in state schools, but he found "the breath of Torquemada" in the suggestion that the state should teach religion for its own ends.[93]

The second speaker added his agreement, and stressed the necessity of church control of secondary education.[94] A third address declared that an adequate religious education could be given apart from any school, and urged the Baptists to rally to the support of state universities.[95] A fourth speaker rejected the idea that Baptists should advocate secular education; "an education that might be given as well in hell as on earth is not that for which Baptists should contend."[96] Other speakers argued that the principles of democracy should be applied to the question, and that the religion of the majority be taught in the schools of the state.[97]

Between the sessions of the Fifth Church Congress and the meeting of the Third National Baptist Educational Convention,

---

[91] *Third Annual Baptist Autumnal Conference*, p. 18. New York: Judson Printing Company, 1885.

[92] *Fifth Annual Session of the Baptist Congress*, p. 62. New York: Baptist Congress Publishing Company, 1887.

[93] *Ibid.*, p. 64.

[94] *Ibid.*, p. 67.

[95] *Ibid.*, p. 70.

[96] *Ibid.*, p. 72.

[97] *Ibid.*, p. 73.

the *Baptist Quarterly Review*, successor to the defunct *Baptist Quarterly*, published several articles on educational topics.[98] The new quarterly, however, never discussed the problem of the control of popular elementary education.

In 1888 occurred the third and final meeting of the National Baptist Educational Convention. At the meeting, which was attended by delegates from thirty-six states, the chairman reported that the Baptist denomination conducted seven seminaries, thirty-eight colleges and universities, and seventy-six academies.[99]

As one of the high lights of the assemblage the convention listened to an address by the Reverend O. P. Eaches on "Resistance to Sectarian Aggression on Common Schools and Public Funds."[100] The aggressive sect was the Catholic Church. The orator posed and answered the question: "Who shall train for citizenship in these elements essential to the well-being of the Republic? I answer: the State."[101] Indeed, church schools cannot properly perform the function of education; the Catholic parochial schools "will give us mutilated men and women."[102] The reason is not far to seek—sectarian doctrine; "children cannot breathe day by day teachings like this, without becoming dwarfed citizens and having their thoughts poisoned against our common country."[103] The control of education does not belong to the church but to the state; and Baptists must emphasize "the need and duty of education by the State for the State."[104]

How far should this state education go? That topic was discussed at the Seventh Baptist Congress. The debate was opened

---

98 *Baptist Quarterly Review*, VIII (1886), pp. 388-89; IX (1887), pp. 63-113, 509-13; X (1888), pp. 348-73.
99 *National Baptist Educational Convention, 1888*, p. 62. Washington: American Baptist Education Society, 1888.
100 *Ibid.*, pp. 27-36.
101 *Ibid.*, p. 31.
102 *Loc. cit.*
103 *Ibid.*, p. 32.
104 *Loc. cit.*

by a demand that the state provide only elementary education.[105] Although the speaker asked this education only for those unable to procure it for themselves, he apparently believed that no one could acquire the rudiments of education without state aid, for he proposed universal compulsory education in the secular schools of the state.[106] The second speaker ignored the set topic of the session to unleash an attack on the Catholic parochial school system.[107]

The Reverend Walter Rauschenbusch found that the state, already in complete control of elementary education, was extending its control upward. Nor did he object; "secular education is passing from the hands of the Church into the hands of the civil power. I believe that tendency is of God."[108] Refusing to accept the arguments for church control of higher education, he declared that they applied equally to primary education, and should end, if accepted, in a system of Baptist parochial schools.[109] Rauschenbusch did not draw the logical conclusion that Baptist secondary schools should be suppressed; rather he called for their improvement. Several other speakers seconded Rauschenbusch's contention that education, secondary as well as primary, was a function not of the church but of the state.[110]

This conclusion was a logical consequence of the Baptist position on the control of elementary education. The earliest Baptist statements on the problem either assume or explicitly state that the control of primary education belongs to the state. Nor was that opinion ever changed. Never, in the present investigation, was there uncovered even a suggestion that the Baptist

---

[105] *Seventh Annual Session of the Baptist Congress*, p. 6. New York: Baptist Congress Publishing Company, 1889.
[106] *Ibid.*, p. 10.
[107] *Ibid.*, pp. 16 ff.
[108] *Ibid.*, p. 30.
[109] *Ibid.*, p. 31.
[110] *Ibid.*, pp. 32, 34.

Church should enter the field of elementary education. The Baptist Church refused to defend the traditional Christian position on the control of primary education. Indeed, its animus against Catholicism led it to formal rejection of the traditional Christian policy. Consequently the Baptist stand demanding a church monopoly of secondary education was untenable. The Baptist denomination rejected the traditional claim of the Christian Church to control popular elementary education; ineluctably, it was compelled to surrender all claims to formal control of secondary education.

CHAPTER VIII

The Churches
Relinquish Control

It is a fact that American Protestantism has relinquished the control of popular elementary education to the state. How great has been the surrender is shown in a recent survey, which found that only four Protestant churches still try to implement the traditional claim of the Christian Church to control elementary education.[1]

The Mennonite denomination has recently revived its parochial schools. It now maintains 18, with an enrollment of 2,500.[2] The Seventh Day Adventists, offspring of the Millerite excitement of the 1840's, conduct 880 elementary schools with 22,000 students.[3] The Christian Reformed Church supports 110 primary schools with about 20,000 pupils.[4]

The Lutheran Synodical Conference, known popularly by the name of its most important section, the Missouri Synod, is the only major Protestant church with a system of parochial schools. It controls the primary education of about 88,000 children in 1,200 schools.[5]

---

[1] Rian, *op. cit.*, pp. 202 ff.
[2] *Ibid.*, p. 210.
[3] *Ibid.*, p. 209.
[4] *Ibid.*, p. 208.
[5] *Ibid.*, p. 202.

In contrast to the 2,500,000 pupils in Catholic parochial schools, less than 150,000 students are receiving their elementary training in Protestant schools in the United States.

Protestantism has abandoned the schools to the state. What were the causes of that surrender?

The present study has presented evidence suggestive of answers to that question from the histories of several major Protestant churches. Before summing up that evidence, however, it would be well to examine the findings of two studies of other important Protestant churches which also created systems of parochial schools.[6] Denominations with at least two thirds of Protestant church membership will then have been seen.

Among the Calvinist churches the major drive for parochial schools took place in the Presbyterian Church. All told, 264 parochial schools were created by the "old-school" Presbyterians.[7] The historian of the movement finds that its rise began in 1846 and its decline in 1854.[8] Before the outbreak of the Civil War the Presbyterian attempt to control popular education was, for all practical purposes, finished.

The causes of the Presbyterian failure will seem familiar to readers of the present study. Sherrill notes that the Presbyterian school system was hastily launched with an inadequate supply of trained teachers.[9] Financial difficulties were not solved. Presbyterians were far from unanimous in their support of the schools; many preferred to send their children to state schools. The General Assembly of the church urged, but it could not order, the creation of schools. Consequently, with the rallying

---

[6] These are Lewis J. Sherrill, *Presbyterian Parochial Schools, 1846-1870* (New Haven: Yale University Press, 1932), and Walter H. Beck, *Lutheran Elementary Schools in the United States* (St. Louis: Concordia Publishing House, 1939).

[7] Sherrill, *op. cit.,* p. 49.

[8] *Ibid.,* p. 51.

[9] *Ibid.,* pp. 174 ff.

of the Presbyterians to "American" schools in preference to "sectarian" schools, the movement failed.

Within the Lutheran denomination in America there were two movements for parochial schools. These drives were motivated, not only by the Lutheran tradition of parochial schools, but by a language problem. Since the worship and literature of Lutheran immigrants were, at least for a generation, in a foreign language, the church had to teach that language to the children or lose them. Indeed, Lutheran schools were commonly known as "German" schools.

Roughly a third of Lutheran church membership today belongs to the United Lutheran Church. This church, theologically the most liberal group in the denomination, traces its origin back to German immigrants in pre-Revolutionary days. These immigrants sparked the drive which led to the creation of over four hundred elementary schools in the colonial and early national period.[10] The drive reached its peak about 1820 and declined quickly thereafter. In the territory of the Pennsylvania Ministerium there were 240 parochial schools in 1820; in 1860 there remained but 28; today there are none.[11]

As the first movement, which took place chiefly in the eastern states, began its decline, the second Lutheran drive for parochial schools began its rise in the Midwest. Again the spark was furnished by German immigrants. Nor did the impetus of the movement slacken until the twentieth century; indeed, Beck calls the years from 1865 to 1900 "the period of major expansion."[12] In the latter years the Lutheran churches were sustaining about 2,500 parochial schools.

By 1936, however, that number had declined to 1,500, of which more than 1,400 were supported by that third of Lutheran

---

10 Beck, *op. cit.*, p. 10.
11 *Ibid.*, p. 74.
12 *Ibid.*, p. 160.

church members who belonged to the Synodical Conference, theologically the most conservative of the Lutheran synods.[13] It was not the schools of the right wing of Lutheranism which had followed those of the left into oblivion, but the schools of the center. Among the synods of the American Lutheran Conference, which includes both Scandinavians and Germans, the most important is the American Lutheran Church, of Germanic origin. It had joined the Missouri Synod in that drive for parochial schools which endured until the end of the nineteenth century. In the twentieth century hundreds of its elementary schools closed their doors, until in 1936 but forty-five remained.[14]

Summarily, while the Lutheran Synodical Conference still maintains its parochial schools, two thirds of the Lutheran denomination, represented by the United Lutheran Church and the American Lutheran Conference, has surrendered the control of popular elementary education to the state. Besides the elements already indicated as operative in other churches, one reason for the relinquishment of the Lutheran schools was the end of the language problem.[15] As the Lutherans adopted English as the language of worship, the need for "German" schools vanished. Consequently the Lutherans turned from the "sectarian" schools of the church to the "American" schools of the state. Beck finds, however, that the principle cause of the decline of Lutheran schools was that "the importance of Christian training had not been fully appreciated. This objective of the school was always paramount; and wherever it was absent, interest and zeal soon waned, and the schools failed to flourish."[16]

Now that every major American denomination has been surveyed, it may be possible to advance some answers to the ques-

---

[13] *Ibid.*, p. 281. It will be remembered that the more recent study of Rian, *op. cit.*, p. 202, found but 1,200 Lutheran elementary schools.

[14] Beck, *op. cit.*, p. 402.

[15] *Ibid.*, pp. 84-85.

[16] *Ibid.*, p. 99.

tion why American Protestantism has relinquished the control of popular elementary education to the state.

To explain that surrender a simplified picture is sometimes drawn of the Protestant dog keeping the Catholic cow away from the manger, while the omnivorous state eats both their dinners. This picture is too simple to be correct. Animus against Catholicism played a part, at times a large part, in forming the educational thought of all the Protestant churches. It seems just to say that anti-Catholicism was the chief factor in the rejection of the traditional Christian position by the Evangelical churches. It cannot be said that opposition to the Catholic Church was the sole or even the major motive in the abandonment of elementary education by the other Protestant churches.

Indeed, while reading the documents of the churches whose efforts to maintain parochial schools failed, one receives the impression that the anti-Catholic canards of their press and congresses were thrown out as a sort of smoke screen behind which the churches could withdraw from an untenable position. Their campaign to control popular elementary education was doomed to defeat by the multiplying common schools of the state, and even more by defections from their own camp. When the signs of defeat were inescapable, the anti-Catholic barrage was begun. When the smoke cleared away, lo! the churches were on the side of the state. They could then persuade themselves that they had really believed all the time that the control of popular education should be vested in the state. Wholeheartedly they could attack the position, so recently held by themselves, but now manned only by the despised Catholics.

Sometimes it is said that behind the movement for universal education lay the Protestant Revolt. Indeed, it would seem that the Protestant stress on the Bible as necessary to eternal salvation would impel the Protestant churches to campaign continually for universal literacy. But the American drive for popular education in the second quarter of the nineteenth century owed little to organized Protestantism. The churches did not, as some educators assert, attack the movement. Neither did they, to any great extent, foster it.

Many of the leaders of that movement were Protestants; some of the most prominent were ministers. A few denominational magazines, particularly in New England, published occasional articles advocating universal education. When it was thought that the common schools were threatened by the Catholics, the Protestant churches could be counted on to rush to their defense. But the organs of opinion of the Protestant churches, whether denominational magazines or congresses, did little to create or popularize the American movement for popular elementary education.

Indeed, the actions of the churches were not so much in support of, as in reaction to, that movement. The movement was largely committed to state control of education; the churches, by the creation of parochial schools, sought to keep that control to themselves.

Each of the four branches of Protestantism had major churches in the United States which endeavored to create systems of parochial schools. The only major Anglican church, the Protestant Episcopal Church, made such an attempt. At one time or another the United Lutherans, the American Lutherans, and the Missouri Synod controlled systems of parochial schools. Among the Calvinists the Presbyterians, the Dutch Reformed, and the German Reformed all made efforts to control popular primary education. Even among the Evangelicals, the Quakers were notable for their parochial schools.

In nineteenth-century America only three major churches did not make an effort to control popular elementary education by establishing church primary schools. These three denominations were the Methodist, the Baptist, and the Congregationalist. Not only were these three churches different from most American denominations in this, but the development of their educational thought had further elements common to the three and different from that of the other American churches.

There were some very rare suggestions in Methodist and Congregationalist organs of opinion that these churches open parochial schools; never did a Baptist make such a suggestion. Never did any of these three churches seriously consider reviving the ancient claim of the church to control popular elementary education. It was in this group that the main effort was made to divide formal education into sections, primary under the state and secondary under the control of the church.

While most American churches, after the failure of their parochial schools, allowed the traditional claim of the church to control popular education to lapse, these three went further by explicitly rejecting that claim. In each of the three cases the rejection of the claim was motivated chiefly by animus against Catholicism, and occurred in attacks on Catholicism.

Anti-Catholicism was also a major motive in other developments in these three churches. It inspired their early demands for the secularization of the state schools. More than other churches, these three approved the state schools as destructive of the faith of Catholic children. More frequently and earlier than other churches, these three hailed the state schools as the only "American" schools, and sanctioned them as Protestant schools. Anti-Catholicism unquestionably was the most important single factor in the evolution of the educational thought of the Methodist, Baptist, and Congregationalist churches in nineteenth-century America.

Yet before the Catholic threat was envisioned, these three churches had already sanctioned the control of popular primary education by the state. How had this come about?

Part of the explanation lies in the fact that the Methodists and Baptists of the second quarter of the nineteenth century were Evangelical sects in an early stage of evolution. Neither church had ever been an established church. Although in the eighteenth century both churches conducted schools, neither church had the century-long traditions of the other churches in control of education, and their brief tradition was forgotten in the generation of neglect of education before the movement for popular education began. Among the Baptists strong elements were hostile or indifferent to education. Again, the Methodists and the Baptists were the Holy Rollers of the second quarter of the nineteenth century. While their membership included educated elements, the great majority of their constituency was of the lower economic classes, poorly educated and largely unconcerned about education.

That the stage of evolution had something to do with the neglect of the church's claim on education by the Methodists and Baptists is indicated by the different history of the only important Evangelical sect to advance the traditional Christian claim, the Quakers. The Society of Friends had, like the other Evangelical churches, never been an established church. But its position, socially and economically, was infinitely superior to that of the Methodists and Baptists. Long before the Methodists and the Baptists, the Quakers had completed the classical evolution of an Evangelical sect into a church of the middle classes, with the traditional middle-class interest in education. The Quakers, financially more able and socially more interested in the education of their children than the Methodists and Baptists, had a much longer tradition of the church control of education. This tradition they maintained in the first quarter of the nineteenth century, while Methodists and Baptists were forgetting their much shorter traditions.

How did it come about that the Congregationalist thought on education during the nineteenth century was so similar to that of the Evangelical Methodists and Baptists? By no stretch of the imagination could the Congregational Church of the nineteenth century be called a primitive Evangelical sect. It had the long Calvinist tradition of church-controlled education. Its membership was largely middle and upper class. It had long been an established church. Yet it, too, rejected the traditional claim of the Christian Church to control popular education.

Undoubtedly, part of the explanation was the proprietary pride that the Congregationalists took in the state schools as creations of Congregationalism. Assuredly another part of the explanation is that, in their New England bailiwick, Congregationalists saw to it that the state schools remained Protestant, if not Congregationalist, schools. Although it neglected formal church control of education, the Congregational Church exercised a very large measure of informal control on the state schools. A third part of the explanation is the weakening of the Calvinistic faith of the Congregationalists and, consequently, of their concern about the transmission of that faith to their children through the medium of elementary schools. As early as the 1820's Unitarian congregations were withdrawing from the Congregational Church; their withdrawal was far from the end of the movement to liberalize the creed of the Puritan Church.

In the course of this study there has been cited a theory which maintains that a main cause of the surrender of the control of popular education by the church was the Evangelical doctrine of conversion. This doctrine teaches that a person becomes a Christian by an instantaneous conversion, which is brought about by the action of the Holy Ghost. It occurs only after the person has reached the age of reason, usually in the teens. Consequently elementary education cannot advance the work of the church.

It is difficult to evaluate the effects of this Evangelical doctrine of conversion on the stand of the Methodists and Baptists on the control of elementary education. While it may have played an influential part—and the connotations of the doctrine are obvious—the present investigation has unearthed little direct evidence to substantiate the theory. Yet it is significant that the group of churches under consideration made the major effort to divide education into sections, the primary under the control of the state and the secondary under the control of the church. This illogical effort was doomed to failure.

In the peculiarly Evangelical doctrine of conversion the Congregationalist, more, probably, than any other non-Evangelical denomination, approached the Baptists and the Methodists. It has already been noted that the four major streams of Protestantism have, in the course of the centuries, commingled. Adumbrations of the doctrine of conversion are found in the Puritan Church as early as Roger Williams and Anne Hutchinson; and the implications of the Half-Way Covenant and the preachings of Jonathan Edwards in the Great Awakening are clear. Indeed, the Evangelical theory of conversion seems to have been dominant in the Congregational Church until it was criticized by Horace Bushnell's *Christian Nurture*, published shortly before the Civil War.

This connection of the Congregationalists with the Methodists and Baptists through the doctrine of conversion may possibly, then, be another reason for the similarity of the development of educational thought in the Evangelical Methodists and Baptists and the Calvinistic Congregationalists.

There were similarities, too, in the history of those Protestant churches which endeavored to implement the traditional claim of the Christian Church to control popular education.

A special element enters the story in the histories of the churches of continental origin, notably the Lutheran and the Reformed. Immigrant members of these churches, accustomed to parochial schools in their native lands, using their native language in their worship, and recognizing the necessity of teaching that language to their children to preserve them in the faith, supported denominational schools. As, with the passing of time, these congregations were Americanized, the need for "German" schools ended. Thereafter the history of their parochial schools is similar to that of other Protestant churches.

This language problem did not exist among the Episcopalians, Presbyterians, Quakers, and the long-established congregations of the Lutheran and Reformed churches. For the most part these churches had neglected elementary education until the drive for popular primary education began in the second quarter of the nineteenth century. Their subsequent efforts to establish systems of parochial schools were, to a great extent, a reaction to the extension of state-controlled primary education.

Apart from the Missouri Synod, the Protestant parochial school systems failed. While the causes of each failure were common to all, it is impossible to determine their relative effects in each church. All that can be said is that these causes were operative in Protestantism's surrender of primary education to the state.

The Protestant parochial schools suffered from a number of deficiencies. The lack of trained teachers was the source of many laments. Unfortunately for the success of their parochial schools, the churches made no effort to recruit teachers or to train them.

Another want was money. As schools became increasingly costly, Protestant congregations showed an increasing unwillingness to shoulder the burden of a double school tax. Apparently Protestant parents were not convinced that the education offered by their churches was superior to that of the state. This lack of conviction was shown by their failure to provide financial support for the church schools—and by their failure to send their children to them.

A third great deficiency of the Protestant schools was a lack of pupils. At times parochial schools failed because the membership of the congregations was so small and scattered that schools were impracticable. Often parochial schools had to close their doors because the children they were established to serve were enrolled in neighboring state schools. This it was that caused the Protestant churches to alter the ideal of a school

beside every church to the objective of church schools in localities devoid of state schools.

The Protestant systems of parochial schools were designed
to keep control of popular elementary education in the hands of
the church and out of the hands of the state. But as the state advanced in the field of education, that control fell almost auto-
matically into its hands. Thus the failure of the Protestant
schools indicates some more fundamental deficiencies, which
caused the lack of teachers and of money and of pupils. These
more radical causes appear to have been a lack of strong interest
in parochial schools, a lack of strong leadership to create and
sustain that interest, and, more fundamental still, a lack of
strong faith in the teachings of their churches which would have
impelled Protestants to see that that faith was inculcated in their
children in schools under the control of their churches.

Increasingly in the nineteenth century, the creeds of Protestantism were called into question. Gradually the new liberal
theology drew adherents away from the old orthodoxies. This
liberalizing movement was most effective at the head of the
churches, among the ministers and influential laymen. It was
just these men who would have to create and sustain interest in
parochial schools if Protestantism was to control popular elementary education. But these men, who were questioning the
Thirty-nine Articles, the Westminster Confession, and the Augs-
burg Confession, saw no need to establish schools to inculcate
these doubtful creeds.

Although strong leadership had initially produced strong
interest, as in the Episcopalian and Presbyterian and Lutheran
churches, that leadership eventually faltered. One of the first
consequences was the collapse of the parochial school system.

The failure of united leadership meant the lack of strong
interest in church schools among the average members of the
congregations. It will be remembered that most efforts to create
Protestant parochial schools occurred only after the average

American Protestant had had time to become accustomed to the common schools. The state had asserted control over popular education. The average American Protestant was quite content to have it so, and this despite the fact that the schools were not perfect and that they were liable to criticism, especially on the point of religion.

When the leaders of his church unanimously called for parochial schools, it would appear that he was ready to follow their guidance. When that leadership wavered, he hesitated. Dutifully, as an American and as a Protestant, he had rallied to the defense of the common school, "godless" as it might be, against alien Catholicism. His denominational organs of opinion began to tell him that the state school was not "godless," but Christian and even Protestant, and above all "American." He was urged to see to it that the common school remained Protestant by retaining the Protestant Bible. The primary education controlled by the state was Protestant. Why should he expend labor and money to create other Protestant schools under the control of the church?

Consequently, American Protestantism surrendered the traditional claim of the Christian Church to control popular elemental education into the hands of the only other claimant, the state. Thus was accomplished a revolutionary change in the history of education and in the history of Christianity.

Denominational Journals and Minutes

THE CONGREGATIONALIST CHURCHES

Minutes of the General Association of Massachusetts [1809-1853].

Minutes of the National Council of Congregational Churches [1871-1895].

Proceedings of the General Convention of Congregational Ministers and Delegates, Albany, 1852. New York: S. W. Benedict, 1852.

Official Record of the National Congregational Council, Boston, 1865. Boston: Congregational Quarterly, 1865.

Debates and Proceedings of the National Council of Congregational Churches, Boston, 1865. Boston: American Congregational Association, 1866.

THE DUTCH REFORMED CHURCH

Acts and Proceedings of the General Synod of the Reformed Protestant Dutch Church [1771-1812].

Acts and Proceedings of the General Synod of the Reformed Dutch Church [1813-1836].

Acts and Proceedings of the General Synod of the Reformed Protestant Dutch Church [1837-1865].

Acts and Proceedings of the General Synod of the Reformed Church in America [1866-1893].

THE GERMAN REFORMED CHURCH

Acts and Proceedings of the General Synod of the German Reformed Church, 1866.

Acts and Proceedings of the General Synod of the Reformed Church in the United States [1869-1899].

THE METHODIST CHURCHES

Minutes Taken at the Several Conferences of the Methodist Episcopal Church in America for 1792. Philadelphia: Parry Hall, 1792.
Journals of the General Conference of the Methodist Episcopal Church [1796-1896].
Journals of the General Conferences of the Methodist Episcopal Church, South [1846-1898].

THE PROTESTANT EPISCOPAL CHURCH

Journals of the General Conventions of the Protestant Episcopal Church [1785-1895].

Other Printed Sources

Address of the Committee of the Laity of the Protestant Episcopal Church, May 31, 1860. New York: The Committee, 1860.
Annual Report of the Board of Education of the Reformed Protestant Dutch Church [32nd-50th]. New York: Board of Publication of Reformed Protestant Dutch Church, 1864-1882.
Asbury, Francis. *Journal of Rev. Francis Asbury: 1771-1815.* 3 vols., New York: Eaton and Mains, n.d.
Burton, Charles E., editor. *National Council Digest.* New York: Executive Committee of the National Council, 1930.
Centennial Papers Published by Order of the General Conference of the Congregational Churches of Connecticut. Hartford: Case, Lockwood and Brainard Company, 1877.
Fifth Annual Session of the Baptist Congress. New York: Baptist Congress Publishing Company, 1887.
Klain, Zora, editor. *Educational Activities of New England Quakers: A Source Book.* Philadelphia: Westbrook Publishing Company, 1928.
Mode, Peter G., editor. *Source Book and Bibliographical Guide for American Church History.* Menasha: Banta Publishing Company, 1921.
National Baptist Educational Convention and Organization of the American Baptist Education Society, Washington, D.C., 1888. Washington: American Baptist Education Society, 1888.
Proceedings of the National Baptist Educational Convention, 1870. New York: Sheldon and Company, 1870.

Proceedings of the National Baptist Educational Convention, 1872.
New York: Sheldon and Company, 1872.
Proceedings of the Second [Episcopal] Church Congress. New York:
Thomas Whittaker, 1876.
Report of the Third [Episcopal] Church Congress. New York: Thomas
Whittaker, 1876.
Richardson, James D., editor. *Messages and Papers of the Presidents.*
20 vols., New York: Bureau of National Literature, 1897-1917.
Seventh Annual Session of the Baptist Congress. New York: Baptist
Congress Publishing Company, 1889.
Sweet, William W., editor. *Religion on the American Frontier.* 4 vols.,
Chicago: University of Chicago Press, 1931-1946.
Third Annual Baptist Autumnal Conference. New York: Judson Print-
ing Company, 1885.
Thorpe, Francis N., editor. *Federal and State Constitutions, Colonial
Charters and Other Organic Laws.* 7 vols., Washington: Govern-
ment Printing Office, 1909.
Woody, Thomas S., editor. *Quaker Education in the Colony and State
of New Jersey: A Source Book.* Philadelphia: University of Penn-
sylvania, 1923.

Periodicals

Baptist Quarterly [1867-1877].
Baptist Quarterly Review [1879-1892].
Bibliotheca Sacra (Congregational quarterly) [1843-1880].
Christian Advocate (Methodist weekly) [1826-1880].
Christian Intelligencer (Dutch Reformed weekly) [1830-1880].
Christian Review (Baptist quarterly) [1836-1863].
Churchman (Episcopalian weekly) [1831-1861; 1867-1880].
Church Review (Episcopalian quarterly) [1848-1885].
Congregational Quarterly [1859-1878].
Examiner (Baptist weekly) [1824-1880].
Ford's Christian Repository (Baptist monthly) [1852-1875].
Independent (Congregational weekly) [1849-1880].
Journal of Christian Education and Family and Sunday School Visiter
(Episcopalian monthly) [1839-1842].
Mercersburg Review (German Reformed quarterly) [1849-1885].

Methodist Quarterly Review [1818-1880].
New Englander (Congregational quarterly) [1843-1880].
Protestant Episcopal Quarterly [1854-1861].
Watchman (Baptist weekly) [1819-1880].

Secondary Works

Adams, Herbert B. *The Church and Popular Education*. Baltimore: Johns Hopkins Press, 1900.

Atkins, Gaius G. and Fagley, Frederick L. *History of American Congregationalism*. Boston: Pilgrim Press, 1942.

Bangs, Nathan. *History of the Methodist Episcopal Church*. 4 vols., New York: Mason and Lane, 1840.

Barclay, Wade C. *Early American Methodism: 1769-1844*. 2 vols., New York: Board of Missions and Church Extension of the Methodist Church, 1949.

Beale, Howard K. *History of Freedom of Teaching in American Schools*. New York: Charles Scribner's Sons, 1941.

Beard, Charles A. and Beard, Mary. *The Rise of American Civilization*, revised edition. 2 vols., New York: The Macmillan Company, 1933.

Beck, Walter H. *Lutheran Elementary Schools in the United States*. St. Louis: Concordia Publishing House, 1939.

Bell, Sadie. *The Church, the State, and Education in Virginia*. New York: Science Press, 1930.

Billington, Ray A. *The Protestant Crusade: 1800-1860*. New York: The Macmillan Company, 1938.

Body, Alfred H. *John Wesley and Education*. London: Epworth Press, 1936.

Bower, William C. *Church and State in Education*. Chicago: University of Chicago Press, 1944.

Brewer, Clifton H. *History of Religious Education in the Episcopal Church to 1835*. New Haven: Yale University Press, 1924.

Brickman, William W. *Guide to Research in Educational History*. New York: New York University Press, 1949.

Brinton, Howard H. *Quaker Education in Theory and Practice*. Wallingford: Pendle Hill Press, 1940.

Brown, Elmer E. *The Making of Our Middle Schools*, third edition. New York: Longmans, Green and Company, 1907.

Brown, Samuel W. *The Secularization of American Education as Shown by State Legislation, State Constitutional Provisions and State Supreme Court Decisions.* New York: Teachers College, Columbia University, 1912.

Brubacher, John S. *History of the Problems of Education.* New York: McGraw-Hill Book Company, 1947.

Carleton, Frank T. *Economic Influences upon Educational Progress, 1820-1850.* Madison: Wisconsin University, 1908.

Chorley, Edward C. *Men and Movements in the American Episcopal Church.* New York: Charles Scribner's Sons, 1946.

Christian, John T. *History of the Baptists.* Nashville: Sunday School Board of Southern Baptist Convention, 1922.

Commons, John and others. *History of Labor in the United States.* 4 vols., New York: The Macmillan Company, 1918-1935.

Confrey, Burton. *Secularism in American Education.* Washington: Catholic University of America, 1931.

Corwin, Charles E. *Manual of the Reformed Church in America: 1628-1922,* fifth edition, revised. New York: Board of Publication and Bible School Work of the Reformed Church in America, 1922.

Corwin, Edwin T. *History of the Reformed Church, Dutch.* New York: Christian Literature Company, 1895.

Cubberley, Elwood P. *History of Education.* Boston: Houghton Mifflin Company, 1920.

———— *Public Education in the United States,* second edition. Boston: Houghton Mifflin Company, 1924.

Culver, Raymond B. *Horace Mann and Religion in the Massachusetts Public Schools.* New Haven: Yale University Press, 1929.

Cummings, A. W. *Early Schools of Methodism.* New York: Phillips and Hunt, 1886.

Curoe, Philip R. V. *Educational Attitudes and Policies of Organized Labor in the United States.* New York: Teachers College, Columbia University, 1926.

Curran, Francis X. *Major Trends in American Church History.* New York: America Press, 1946.

Curti, Merle. *The Social Ideas of American Educators.* New York: Charles Scribner's Sons, 1935.

Dobbs, Joseph H. *The Reformed Church, German*. New York: Christian Literature Company, 1895.

Draper, Andrew S. *American Education*. Boston: Houghton Mifflin Company, 1909.

Dunlap, William C. *Quaker Education in Baltimore and Virginia Yearly Meetings*. Philadelphia: The Author, 1936.

Dunning, Albert E. *The Congregationalists in America*. Boston: Pilgrim Press, 1894.

Duvall, Sylvanus M. *The Methodist Episcopal Church and Education up to 1869*. New York: Teachers College, Columbia University, 1929.

Edwards, Newton and Richey, Herman G. *The School in the American Social Order*. Boston: Houghton Mifflin Company, 1947.

Elsbree, Willard S. *The American Teacher*. New York: American Book Company, 1939.

Fleming, Sanford. *Children and Puritanism*. New Haven: Yale University Press, 1933.

Gabel, Richard J. *Public Funds for Church and Private Schools*. Washington: Catholic University of America, 1937.

Godbold, Albea. *The Church College of the Old South*. Durham: Duke University Press, 1944.

Gorrie, P. Douglass. *Episcopal Methodism*, fourth edition. Auburn: Miller, Orton and Mulligan, 1854.

Greene, Evarts B. *Religion and the State*. New York: New York University Press, 1941.

Hall, Arthur J. *Religious Education in the Public Schools of the City and State of New York*. Chicago: University of Chicago Press, 1914.

Hansen, Allen O. *Liberalism and American Education in the Eighteenth Century*. New York: The Macmillan Company, 1926.

Hinsdale, B. A. *Horace Mann and the Common School Revival in the United States*. New York: Charles Scribner's Sons, 1898.

Jackson, Sidney. *America's Struggle for Free Schools*. Washington: American Council on Public Affairs, 1941.

Johnson, Alvin W. *Legal Status of Church-State Relationships in the United States, with Special Reference to the Public Schools*. Minneapolis: University of Minnesota, 1934.

Johnson, Alvin W. and Yost, Frank H. *Separation of Church and State in the United States.* Minneapolis: University of Minnesota Press, 1948.

Klain, Zora. *Quaker Contributions to Education in North Carolina.* Philadelphia: The Author, 1924.

Knight, Edgar W. *Education in the United States,* new edition. Boston: Ginn and Company, 1934.

Landis, Benson Y., editor. *Yearbook of American Churches, 1943.* Lebanon: Sowers Printing Company, 1943.

Lewis, Frank G. *A Sketch of the History of Baptist Education in Pennsylvania.* Chester: Crozer Theological Seminary, 1919.

Limbert, Paul M. *Denominational Policies in the Support and Supervision of Higher Education.* New York: Teachers College, Columbia University, 1929.

Magruder, Edith C. *A Historical Study of the Educational Agencies of the Southern Baptist Convention, 1845-1945.* New York: Teachers College, Columbia University, 1951.

Manross, William W. *The Episcopal Church in the United States, 1800-1840.* New York: Columbia University Press, 1938.

———— *History of the American Episcopal Church.* Milwaukee: Morehouse Publishing Company, 1935.

Martin, George H. *Evolution of the Massachusetts Public School System.* New York: D. Appleton and Company, 1894.

McConnell, S. D. *History of the American Episcopal Church,* tenth edition. Milwaukee: Young Churchman Company, 1916.

Moehlman, Conrad. *School and Church: The American Way.* New York: Harper and Brothers, 1944.

Monroe, Paul. *Founding of the American Public School System.* New York: The Macmillan Company, 1940.

Mott, Frank L. *History of American Magazines, 1741-1850.* 3 vols., New York: D. Appleton-Century Company, 1930-1938.

Newman, Albert H., editor. *A Century of Baptist Achievement.* Philadelphia: American Baptist Publication Society, 1901.

Newman, Albert H. *History of the Baptist Churches in the United States,* sixth edition, revised and enlarged. Philadelphia: American Baptist Publication Society, 1915.

Noble, Stuart G. *History of American Education.* New York: Farrar and Rinehart, 1938.

O'Connell, Geoffrey. *Naturalism in American Education.* New York: Benziger Brothers, 1938.

Peck, George. *Life and Times of George Peck.* New York: Nelson and Phillips, 1874.

Perry, William S. *History of the American Episcopal Church, 1587-1883.* 2 vols., Boston: Osgood, 1885.

Piette, Maximin. *John Wesley in the Evolution of Protestantism.* New York: Sheed and Ward, 1937.

Reisner, Edward H. *Evolution of the Common School.* New York: The Macmillan Company, 1930.

——— *Nationalism and Education since 1789.* New York: The Macmillan Company, 1922.

Rian, Edwin H. *Christianity and American Education.* San Antonio: Naylor Company, 1949.

Ridgway, Henry B. *Edmund S. Janes.* New York: Phillips and Hunt, 1882.

Russell, Elbert. *History of Quakerism.* New York: The Macmillan Company, 1942.

Schaff, Philip and others, editors. *The American Church History Series.* 13 vols., New York: Christian Literature Company, 1893-1901.

Schneider, Carl E. *The German Church on the American Frontier.* St. Louis: Eden Publishing House, 1939.

Sherrill, Lewis J. *Presbyterian Parochial Schools, 1846-1870.* New Haven: Yale University Press, 1932.

Sperry, Willard L. *Religion in America.* New York: The Macmillan Company, 1946.

Stevens, Abel. *History of the Methodist Episcopal Church in the United States.* 4 vols., New York: Carlton and Porter, 1866-1867.

Stewart, George. *History of Religious Education in Connecticut to 1850.* New Haven: Yale University Press, 1924.

Tewksbury, Donald G. *The Founding of American Colleges and Universities before the Civil War, with Particular Reference to the Religious Influences Bearing upon the College Movement.* New York: Teachers College, Columbia University, 1932.

Thayer, Vivian T. *Religion in Public Education.* New York: The Viking Press, 1947.

Tiffany, Charles C. *History of the Protestant Episcopal Church*, third edition. New York: Charles Scribner's Sons, 1903.

Vedder, Henry C. *The Baptists*. New York: Baker and Taylor Company, 1903.

────── *History of the Baptists in the Middle States.* Philadelphia: American Baptist Publication Society, 1898.

────── *Short History of the Baptists*, new edition. Philadelphia: American Baptist Publication Society, 1907.

Walker, Williston. *A History of the Congregational Churches in the United States*, fifth edition. New York: Charles Scribner's Sons, 1900.

Wilberforce, Samuel. *History of the Protestant Episcopal Church*, second edition. London: Rivington and Company, 1846.

Wilson, Carl B. *The Baptist Manual Labor School Movement in the United States*. Waco: Baylor University Press, 1937.

Woody, Thomas S. *Early Quaker Education in Pennsylvania*. New York: Teachers College, Columbia University, 1920.

Zollman, Carl. *American Church Law*, second edition. St. Paul: West Publishing Company, 1933.

Doctoral Dissertations

Sherrill, Lewis J. *Parochial Schools in the Old South Presbyterian Church*. Yale University, 1929.

Stauffer, Alvin P. *Anti-Catholicism in American Politics, 1865-1900*. Harvard University, 1933.

INDEX